Fodor's 1st

Pocket
Aruba

Reprinted from *Fodor's Caribbean*

Fodor's Travel Publications, Inc.
New York • Toronto • London • Sydney • Auckland
www.fodors.com/

Fodor's Pocket Aruba

EDITORS: Caroline V. Haberfeld, Christina Knight

Editorial Contributors: Robert Andrews, Robert Blake, David Brown, Melissa Rivers, Heidi Sarna, Helayne Schiff, M. T. Schwartzman (Gold Guide editor), Dinah A. Spritzer
Editorial Production: Tracy Patruno
Maps: David Lindroth *cartographer*; Robert Blake, *map editor*
Design: Fabrizio La Rocca, *creative director*; Guido Caroti, *associate art director*; Jolie Novak, *photo editor*
Production/Manufacturing: Mike Costa
Cover Photograph: Bob Krist

Copyright

ISBN 0–679–03608–3

First Edition

Special Sales

PRINTED IN THE UNITED STATES OF AMERICA

10 9 8 7 6 5 4 3 2 1

CONTENTS

Maps

ON THE ROAD WITH FODOR'S

WE'RE **ALWAYS THRILLED** to get letters from readers, especially one like this:

It took us an hour to decide what book to buy and we now know we picked the best one. Your book was wonderful, easy to follow, very accurate, and good on pointing out eating places, informal as well as formal. When we saw other people using your book, we would look at each other and smile.

Our editors and writers are deeply committed to making every Fodor's guide "the best one"—not only accurate but always charming, brimming with sound recommendations and solid ideas, right on the mark in describing restaurants and hotels, and full of fascinating facts that make you view what you've traveled to see in a rich new light.

About Our Writer

Our success in achieving our goals—and in helping to make your trip the best of all possible vacations—is a credit to the hard work of our extraordinary writers.

Melissa Rivers spends her summers in Alaska and Canada, and her winters island-hopping in the Caribbean on assignment for Fodor's and other publications. She likes getting off the beaten paths and especially enjoys diving and snorkeling in the ABCs (Aruba, Bonaire, Curaçau). She has also contributed to several Fodor's guides: *Alaska, Canada, Caribbean, USA, Worldwide Cruises and Ports of Call, Great American Learning Vacations,* and *Great American Sports and Adventure Vacations.*

New This Year

On the Web, check out Fodor's site (www.fodors.com/) for information on major destinations around the world and travel-savvy interactive features. The Web site also lists the 85-plus stations nationwide that carry the *Fodor's Travel Show,* a live radio call-in program that airs every weekend. Tune in to hear guests discuss their wonderful adventures—or call in to get answers for your most pressing travel questions.

We're also proud to announce that the American Society of Travel Agents has endorsed Fodor's as its guidebook of choice. ASTA is the world's largest and most influential travel trade association, operating in more than 170 countries, with 27,000 members pledged to adhere to a strict code of ethics reflecting the Society's motto, "Integrity in Travel." ASTA shares Fodor's devotion to providing smart, honest travel information and advice to travelers, and we've long recommended that our readers consult ASTA member agents for the experience and professionalism they bring to the table.

How to Use This Book

Organization

Up front is **Essential Information,** an easy-to-use section divided alphabetically by topic. Under each listing you'll find tips and information that will help you accomplish what you need to in Aruba. You'll also find addresses and telephone numbers of organizations and companies that offer destination-related services and detailed information and publications.

The first chapter in the guide, **Destination: Aruba,** helps get you in the mood for your trip and alerts you to festivals and seasonal events you'll want to seek out.

The following chapters cover lodging, dining, beaches, outdoor activities and sports, shopping, nightlife, and exploring in Aruba. Chapter 8 focuses on the nearby island **Curaçao** and includes information on exploring, beaches, dining, shopping, and how to get there from Aruba.

The last chapter, **A Gambling Primer,** will help you to prepare your strategy for Aruban casinos.

Icons and Symbols

★ Our special recommendations

✕ Restaurant

🏨 Lodging establishment

🐤 Good for kids (rubber duckie)

☞ Sends you to another section of the guide for more information

✉ Address

☎ Telephone number

⏲ Opening and closing times

🎫 Admission prices (those we give apply to adults; substantially reduced fees are almost always available for children, students, and senior citizens)

Hotel Facilities

We always list the facilities that are available—but we don't specify whether they cost extra: When pricing accommodations, always ask what's included. In addition, assume that all rooms have private baths unless otherwise noted.

There are numerous meal plans offered in Aruba: **European Plan** (EP, with no meals), **Full American Plan** (FAP, with all meals), **Modified American Plan** (MAP, with breakfast and dinner daily), **Continental Plan** (CP, with a Continental breakfast daily), andr **All-inclusive** (all meals and most activities). At the end of each lodging review, we've listed the meal plans the hotel offers.

A Full American Plan may be ideal for travelers on a budget who don't want to worry about additional expenses, but travelers who enjoy a different dining experience each night will prefer to book rooms on the European Plan. Since some hotels insist on the Modified American Plan, particularly during the high season, you might want to find out whether you can exchange dinner for lunch or for meals at neighboring hotels.

Restaurant Reservations and Dress Codes

Reservations are always a good idea; we note only when they're essential or when they are not accepted. Book as far ahead as you can, and reconfirm when you get to town. Unless otherwise noted, the restaurants listed are open daily for lunch and dinner. We mention dress only when men are required to wear a jacket or a jacket and tie.

Credit Cards

The following abbreviations are used: **AE,** American Express; **D,** Discover; **DC,** Diners Club; **MC,** MasterCard; and **V,** Visa.

Don't Forget to Write

You can use this book in the confidence that all prices and opening times are based on information supplied to us at press time; Fodor's cannot accept responsibility for any errors. Time in-

evitably brings changes, so always confirm information when it matters—especially if you're making a detour to visit a specific place. In addition, when making reservations be sure to mention if you have a disability or are traveling with children, if you prefer a private bath or a certain type of bed, or if you have specific dietary needs or other concerns.

Were the restaurants we recommended as described? Did our hotel picks exceed your expectations? Did you find a museum we recommended a waste of time? If you have complaints, we'll look into them and revise our entries when the facts warrant it. If you've discovered a special place that we haven't included, we'll pass the information along to our correspondents and have them check it out. So send us your feedback, positive *and* negative: email us at editors@fodors.com (specify the name of the book on the subject line) or write the Aruba editor at Fodor's, 201 East 50th Street, New York, New York 10022. Have a wonderful trip!

Karen Cure
Editorial Director

The Caribbean

THE BAHAMAS

Turks
and
Caicos
Islands

Cuba

Dominican
Republic

Haiti

Hispaniola

G R E A T E R

Port-au-
Prince

Santo
Domingo

Jamaica

A N T I L L

N

Caribbean

| 0 | | 200 miles |
| 0 | | 300 km |

Aruba

Bonaire

Willemstad

Curaçao

COLOMBIA   Maracaibo

VENEZUELA

Carac

ATLANTIC OCEAN

LEEWARD ISLANDS

St. John
St. Thomas
Virgin Gorda
Tortola
Anguilla
San Juan
St. Maarten/
St. Martin
St. Barthélemy
Saba
Barbuda
Puerto
Rico
St.
Croix
St. Eustatius
Antigua
St. Kitts
Nevis
Montserrat
Marie
Galante
Guadeloupe
ILLES
WINDWARD ISLANDS
Dominica
Martinique
Fort-de-France
Sea
St. Lucia
Barbados
St. Vincent
Bridgetown
The
Grenadines
St. George's
Grenada
Tobago
onaire
LESSER ANTILLES
Trinidad
Caracas

ESSENTIAL INFORMATION

*Basic Information on Traveling in Aruba,
Savvy Tips to Make Your Trip a Breeze, and
Companies and Organizations to Contact*

AIR TRAVEL

Queen Beatrix International Airport is on Aruba's south coast, just east of the capital, Oranjestad. Aruba is a 2½-hour flight from Miami and a four-hour flight from New York.

Flights to Aruba leave daily from New York–area airports and from Miami International Airport, with easy connections from most other American cities. Always **bring a photo ID to the airport.** You may be asked to show it before you are allowed to check in.

Air Aruba, the island's official airline, flies nonstop to Aruba daily from Miami and Newark. Twice-weekly service departs from Baltimore. American Airlines offers daily nonstop service from both Miami and New York and connecting flights from several U.S. cities via San Juan. ALM, the major airline of the Dutch Caribbean islands, flies six days a week nonstop from Miami and twice weekly from Fort Lauderdale to Aruba. Air Aruba and ALM also have connecting flights to Caracas, Bonaire, Curaçao, and St. Maarten as well as other Caribbean islands. ALM also of-fers the Visit Caribbean Pass for interisland travel.

ARUBA'S AIRPORT➤ **Queen Beatrix Airport** (☎ 297/8–24829).

AIRLINES➤ **Air Aruba** (☎ 297/8–23151 or 800/862–7822). **American Airlines** (☎ 297/8–22006 or 800/433–7300). **ALM** (☎ 297/8–23546 or 800/327–7230).

FROM CANADA➤ **Air Canada** (☎ 246/428–5077 or 800/776–3000). **American Airlines** (☎ 800/433–7300).

FROM THE U.K➤ **British Airways** (☎ 0345/222–111), **British West Indian Airways** (☎ 0181/570–5552), and **Caledonian** (☎ 01293/567–100) are the only airlines with direct flights from London to the Caribbean.

THE LOWEST FARE

The least-expensive airfares to Aruba are priced for round-trip travel. Major airlines usually require that you **book far in advance and stay at least seven days** and no more than 30 to get the lowest fares. Ask about ultrasaver fares, which are the cheapest; they must be booked 90 days in advance and are nonrefundable. A little more expensive are supersaver fares, which require only a 30-day advance purchase. Remember that penalties for refunds or scheduling changes are stiffer for international tickets, usually about $150. International flights are also sensitive to the season: **plan to fly in the off season** for the cheapest fares. If your destination or home city has more than one gateway, **compare prices to and from different airports.** Also price flights scheduled for off-peak hours, which may be significantly less expensive.

To save money on flights from the United Kingdom and back, **look into an APEX or Super-PEX ticket.** APEX tickets must be booked in advance and have certain restrictions. Super-PEX tickets can be purchased at the airport on the day of departure—subject to availability.

AGENTS

Travel agents, especially those who specialize in finding the lowest fares, can be especially helpful when booking a plane ticket. When you're quoted a price, **ask your agent if the price is likely to get any lower.** Good agents know the seasonal fluctuations of airfares and can usually anticipate a sale or fare war. However, waiting can be risky: The fare could go *up* as seats become scarce, and you may wait so long that your preferred flight sells out. A wait-and-see strategy works best if your plans are flexible, but if you must

arrive and depart on certain dates, don't delay.

CONSOLIDATORS

Consolidators buy tickets for scheduled flights at reduced rates from the airlines then sell them at prices that beat the best fare available directly from the airlines, usually without advance restrictions. Sometimes you can even get your money back if you need to return the ticket. Carefully read the fine print detailing penalties for changes and cancellations, and **confirm your consolidator reservation with the airline.**

CONSOLIDATORS➤ **United States Air Consolidators Association** (✉ 925 L St., Suite 220, Sacramento, CA 95814, ☎ 916/441–4166, FAX 916/441–3520).

GETTING BUMPED

Airlines routinely overbook planes, knowing that not everyone with a ticket will show up, but sometimes everyone does. When that happens, airlines ask for volunteers to give up their seats. In return, these volunteers usually get a certificate for a free flight and are rebooked on the next flight out. If there are not enough volunteers, the airline must choose who will be denied boarding. The first to get bumped are passengers who checked in late and those flying on discounted tickets, **so get to the gate and check in as early as possible,** especially during peak periods.

ENJOY THE FLIGHT

For more legroom, **request an emergency-aisle seat**; however, don't sit in the row in front of the emergency aisle or in front of a bulkhead, where seats may not recline. If you don't like airline food, **ask for special meals when booking.** These can be vegetarian, low-cholesterol, or kosher, for example. Some carriers have prohibited smoking throughout their systems; others allow smoking only on certain routes or even certain departures from that route, so **contact your carrier regarding its smoking policy.**

COMPLAINTS

If your baggage goes astray or your flight goes awry, **complain right away.** Most carriers require that you file a claim immediately.

AIRLINE COMPLAINTS➤ U.S. Department of Transportation **Aviation Consumer Protection Division** (⊠ C-75, Washington, DC 20590, ☎ 202/366-2220). **Federal Aviation Administration (FAA) Consumer Hotline** (☎ 800/322-7873).

AIRPORT TRANSPORTATION

Many car-rental agencies (☞ Car Rental) have offices at Aruba's airport. The taxi fare to Oranjested is about $10, to low-rise hotels about $15, and to high-rise hotels about $17.

BICYCLE, MOPED, & MOTORCYCLE RENTALS

Rates vary according to the make of the vehicle; expect to pay around $20 for an 80CC to $40 for a 250CC.

RENTALS➤ **George's Cycle Center** (⊠ L. G. Smith Blvd. 136D, ☎ 297/8-25975) for Yamaha scooters. **Ron's Motorcycle Rental** (⊠ Bakval 17A, ☎ 297/8-62090). **Nelson Motorcycle Rental** (⊠ Gasparito 10A, ☎ 297/8-66801). **New York Cycles and Scooters** (⊠ Noord 76, ☎ 297/8-63885). **Semver Cycle Rental** (⊠ Noord 22, ☎ 297/8-66851). **Pablito's Bike Rental** (⊠ L. G. Smith Blvd. 234, ☎ 297/8-78655) rents mountain bikes for $10 per day.

BOATING

YACHT CHARTERS➤ **Alden Yacht Charters** (⊠ 1909 Alden Landing, Portsmouth, RI 02871, ☎ 401/683-1782 or 800/662-2628, FAX 401/683-3668). **Huntley Yacht Vacations** (⊠ 210 Preston Rd., Wernersville, PA 19565, ☎ 610/678-2628 or 800/322-9224, FAX 610/670-1767). **Lynn Jachney Charters** (⊠ Box 302, Marblehead, MA 01945, 617/639-0787 or 800/223-2050, FAX 617/639-0216). **Nicholson Yacht Charters** (⊠ 78 Bolton St., Cambridge, MA 02140-3321, ☎ 617/661-0555 or 800/662-6066, FAX 617/661-0554). **Ocean Voyages** (⊠ 1709 Bridgeway, Sausalito, CA 94965, ☎ 415/332-4681 or 800/299-4444, FAX 415/332-7460). **Russell Yacht Charters** (⊠ 404 Hulls Hwy., #175, Southport, CT 06490, ☎ 203/255-2783 or 800/635-8895). **SailAway Yacht**

Charters (⊠ 15605 S.W. 92nd Ave., Miami, FL 33157-1972, ☎ 305/253-7245 or 800/724-5292, FAX 305/251-4408).

BUS TRAVEL

Buses run hourly trips between the beach hotels and Oranjestad. One-way fare is $1; **pay with exact change.** Buses also run down the coast from Oranjestad to San Nicolas for the same fare. Contact the Aruba Tourism Authority (☎ 297/8-21019) for a bus schedule, or inquire at the front desk of your hotel.

CAR RENTAL

The island's winding roads are poorly marked, if at all (though this is slowly changing as the government installs new road signs and more clearly mark sights of interest). The major tourist attractions are fairly easy to find; others you'll happen upon only by sheer luck (or with an Aruban friend). If you plan to explore the island's natural sights, **opt for a four-wheel-drive vehicle.**

Rental rates are between $50 and $65 per day. Insurance is available starting at $10 per day, and all companies offer unlimited mileage. Local car-rental companies generally have lower rates. **Make reservations before visiting the island.**

LOCAL AGENCIES➤ **Avis** (⊠ Kolibristraat 14, ☎ 297/8-28787; ⊠ Airport, ☎ 297/8-25496). **Bud-**get Rent-a-Car (⊠ Kolibristraat 1, ☎ 297/8-2860). **Hertz, De Palm Car Rental** (⊠ L. G. Smith Blvd. 142, Box 656, ☎ 297/8-24545; ⊠ Airport, ☎ 297/8-24886). **Dollar Rent-a-Car** (⊠ Grendeaweg 15, ☎ 297/8-22783; ⊠ Airport, ☎ 297/8-25651; ⊠ Manchebo, ☎ 297/8-26696). **National** (⊠ Tanki Leendert 170, ☎ 297/8-21967; ⊠ Airport, ☎ 297/8-25451). **Thrifty** (⊠ Balashi 65, ☎ 297/8-55300; ⊠ Airport, ☎ 297/8-35335). **Hedwina Car Rental** (⊠ Bubali 93A, ☎ 297/8-76442; ⊠ Airport, ☎ 297/8-30880).

MAJOR AGENCIES➤ **Alamo** (☎ 800/522-9696, 0800/272-2000 in the U.K.). **Avis** (☎ 800/331-1084, 800/879-2847 in Canada) rents to drivers over 23. **Budget** (☎ 800/472-3325, 0800/181181 in the U.K.) rents to drivers over 25. **Dollar** (☎ 800/800-4000; 0990/565656 in the U.K., where it is known as Eurodollar). **Hertz** (☎ 800/654-3001, 800/263-0600 in Canada, 0345/555888 in the U.K.) rents to drivers over 21. **National InterRent** (☎ 800/227-3876; 01345/222525 in the U.K., where it is known as Europcar InterRent).

CUT COSTS

To get the best deal, **book through a travel agent who is willing to shop around.**

Also **ask your travel agent about a company's customer-service**

record. How has it responded to late plane arrivals and vehicle mishaps? Are there often lines at the rental counter, and if you're traveling during a holiday period, does a confirmed reservation guarantee you a car?

NEED INSURANCE?

When driving a rented car, you are generally responsible for any damage to or loss of the vehicle. You also are liable for any property damage or personal injury that you may cause while driving. Before you rent, **see what coverage you already have** under the terms of your personal auto-insurance policy and credit cards.

BEWARE SURCHARGES

Before you pick up a car in one city and leave it in another, **ask about drop-off charges or one-way service fees,** which can be substantial. Note, too, that some rental agencies charge extra if you return the car before the time specified on your contract. To avoid a hefty refueling fee, **fill the tank just before you turn in the car,** but be aware that gas stations near the rental outlet may overcharge.

MEET THE REQUIREMENTS

You'll need a valid U.S. or Canadian driver's license or an International Driver's Permit held for at least two years to rent a car, and you must be able to meet the minimum age requirements of each rental service, implemented for in-

surance reasons. A deposit of US$500 or a signed credit card slip is also required.

CUSTOMS & DUTIES

When shopping, **keep receipts** for all of your purchases. Upon reentering the country, **be ready to show customs officials what you've bought.** If you feel a duty is incorrect, appeal the assessment. If you object to the way your clearance was handled, get the inspector's badge number. In either case, first ask to see a supervisor, then write to the port director at the address listed on your receipt. Send a copy of the receipt and other appropriate documentation. If you still don't get satisfaction, you can take your case to customs headquarters in Washington, D.C.

ENTERING ARUBA

In addition to personal-use items, travelers 18 and over may bring in 2 liters of liquor and 200 cigarettes, 50 cigars, and 250 grams of tobacco. Dogs and cats (which aren't allowed at most hotels) can enter with a valid rabies and health certificate issued by a recognized veterinarian. Pets from South and Central America are not allowed.

ENTERING THE U.S.

You may bring home $600 worth of foreign goods duty-free if you've been out of the country for at least 48 hours and haven't used the $600 allowance or any part of it in the past 30 days. This allowance, higher than the standard $400 exemption, applies to Aruba and the two dozen countries included in the Caribbean Basin Initiative (CBI). If you also visit a non-CBI country, such as Martinique, you may still bring in $600 worth of goods duty-free, but no more than $400 may be from the non-CBI country. If your travel included the U.S. Virgin Islands (USVI), a $1,200 allowance applies, but at least $600 worth of goods must be from the USVI.

Travelers 21 and older may bring back 1 liter of alcohol duty-free. In addition, regardless of your age, you are allowed 200 cigarettes and 100 non-Cuban cigars. (At press time, a federal rule restricting tobacco access to persons 18 years and older did not apply to importation.) Antiques, which the U.S. Customs Service defines as objects more than 100 years old, enter duty-free, as do original works of art done entirely by hand, including paintings, drawings, and sculptures.

You may also send packages home duty-free: up to $200 worth of goods for personal use, with a limit of one parcel per addressee per day (and no alcohol or tobacco products or perfume worth more than $5); label the package PER-SONAL USE and attach a list of its contents and their retail value. Do not label the package UNSOLICITED GIFT, or your duty-free exemption will drop to $100. Mailed items do not affect your duty-free allowance on your return.

INFORMATION➤ **U.S. Customs Service** (✉ Box 7407, Washington, DC 20044, ☏ 202/927–6724); complaints (✉ Commissioner's Office, 1301 Constitution Ave. NW, Washington, DC 20229); registration of equipment (✉ Resource Management, 1301 Constitution Ave. NW, Washington DC, 20229, ☏ 202/927–0540).

ENTERING CANADA

If you've been out of Canada for at least seven days, you may bring in C$500 worth of goods duty-free. If you've been away for fewer than seven days but more than 48 hours, the duty-free allowance drops to C$200; if your trip lasts 24–48 hours, the allowance is C$50. You may not pool allowances with family members. Goods claimed under the C$500 exemption may follow you by mail; those claimed under the lesser exemptions must accompany you.

Alcohol and tobacco products may be included in the seven-day and 48-hour exemptions but not in the 24-hour exemption. If you meet the age requirements of the province or territory through which you reenter Canada, you may bring in duty-free 1.14 liters (40 imperial ounces) of wine or liquor or 24 12-ounce cans or bottles of beer or ale. If you are 16 or older, you may bring in duty-free

200 cigarettes and 50 cigars; these items must accompany you.

You may send an unlimited number of gifts worth up to C$60 each duty-free to Canada. Label the package UNSOLICITED GIFT—VALUE UNDER $60. Alcohol and tobacco are excluded.

INFORMATION➤ **Revenue Canada** (✉ 2265 St. Laurent Blvd. S, Ottawa, Ontario K1G 4K3, ☎ 613/993−0534, 800/461−9999 in Canada).

ENTERING THE U.K.

From countries outside the EU, including Aruba, you may import duty-free 200 cigarettes or 50 cigars, 1 liter of spirits or 2 liters of fortified or sparkling wine or liqueurs, 2 liters of still table wine, 60 milliliters of perfume, 250 milliliters of toilet water, plus £136 worth of other goods, including gifts and souvenirs.

INFORMATION➤ **HM Customs and Excise** (✉ Dorset House, Stamford St., London SE1 9NG, ☎ 0171/202−4227).

ELECTRICITY

Electricity operates on 110 volts, 60 cycles, the same as in the United States. If your appliances are dual-voltage, you'll need only an adapter. Don't use 110-volt outlets, marked FOR SHAVERS ONLY, for high-wattage appliances such as blow-dryers. Most laptops operate equally well on 110 and 220 volts and so require only an adapter.

EMERGENCIES

All hotels have house doctors on call 24 hours a day; call the front desk.

Police (☎ 11000). **Ambulance and Fire** (☎ 115). **Dr. Horacio Oduber Hospital** (☎ 74300, FAX 73348). **Pharmacy** (✉ Botica del Pueblo, ☎ 22154).

HEALTH

Sunburn and sunstroke can be serious. A long-sleeve shirt, a hat, and long pants or a beach wrap are essential on a boat, for midday at the beach, and whenever you go out sightseeing. **Use sunblock lotion** on nose, ears, and other sensitive areas, **limit your sun time** for the first few days, and be sure to **drink enough liquids.** The water on the island is desalinated and purified, so it is safe for drinking.

Divers' alert: **Do not fly within 24 hours of scuba diving.**

HOURS

Shops are generally open 8−noon and 2−6, Monday through Saturday. Some stores stay open through the lunch hours, noon−2, and many open when cruise ships are in port on Sunday and holidays. Nighttime shopping at the Alhambra Bazaar runs 5−midnight. Bank hours are weekdays 8−noon and 1:30−4. The Aruba Bank at the airport is open Saturday from 9 to 4 and Sunday from 9 to 1.

INSURANCE

Travel insurance is the best way to **protect yourself against financial loss.** The most useful policies are trip-cancellation-and-interruption, default, medical, and comprehensive insurance.

Without insurance you will lose all or most of your money if you cancel your trip, regardless of the reason. It's essential that you **buy trip-cancellation-and-interruption insurance,** particularly if your airline ticket, cruise, or package tour is nonrefundable and cannot be changed. When considering how much coverage you need, look for a policy that will cover the cost of your trip plus the nondiscounted price of a one-way airline ticket, should you need to return home early. Also **consider default or bankruptcy insurance,** which protects you against a supplier's failure to deliver.

Medicare generally does not cover health-care costs outside the United States, nor do many privately issued policies. If your own policy does not cover you outside the United States, **consider buying supplemental medical coverage.** Remember that travel health insurance is different from a medical-assistance plan.

Citizens of the United Kingdom can buy an annual travel-insurance policy valid for most vacations during the year in which it's purchased. If you are pregnant or have a preexisting medical condition, make sure you're covered.

If you have purchased an expensive vacation, particularly one that involves travel abroad, comprehensive insurance is a must. **Look for comprehensive policies that include trip-delay insurance,** which will protect you in the event that weather problems cause you to miss your flight, tour, or cruise. A few insurers sell waivers for preexisting medical conditions. Companies that offer both features include Access America, Carefree Travel, Travel Insured International, and Travel Guard (☞ *below*).

Always **buy travel insurance directly from the insurance company**; if you buy it from a travel agency or tour operator that goes out of business, you probably will not be covered for the agency or operator's default, a major risk. Before you make any purchase, **review your existing health and home-owner's policies** to find out whether they cover expenses incurred while traveling.

U.S. TRAVEL INSURERS➤ **Access America** (⊠ 6600 W. Broad St., Richmond, VA 23230, ☎ 804/285–3300 or 800/284–8300). **Carefree Travel Insurance** (⊠ Box 9366, 100 Garden City Plaza, Garden City, NY 11530, ☎ 516/294–0220 or 800/323–3149).

Near Travel Services (⊠ Box 1339, Calumet City, IL 60409, ☎ 708/868–6700 or 800/654–6700). **Travel Guard International** (⊠ 1145 Clark St., Stevens Point, WI 54481, ☎ 715/345–0505 or 800/826–1300). **Travel Insured International** (⊠ Box 280568, East Hartford, CT 06128-0568, ☎ 860/528–7663 or 800/243–3174). **Travelex Insurance Services** (⊠ 11717 Burt St., Suite 202, Omaha, NE 68154-1500, ☎ 402/445–8637 or 800/228–9792, FAX 800/867–9531). **Wallach & Company** (⊠ 107 W. Federal St., Box 480, Middleburg, VA 20118, ☎ 540/687–3166 or 800/237–6615).

IN CANADA➤ **Mutual of Omaha** (⊠ Travel Division, 500 University Ave., Toronto, Ontario M5G 1V8, ☎ 416/598–4083, 800/268–8825 in Canada).

IN THE U.K.➤ **Association of British Insurers** (⊠ 51 Gresham St., London EC2V 7HQ, ☎ 0171/600–3333).

LANGUAGE

The native language in Aruba is Papiamento, a creole dialect made up of Dutch, Spanish, English, French, Portuguese, Arawak, and several African languages. The dialect makes sense for a small population that traces its ancestry to over 40 different ethnic groups. The island's official language is Dutch, but most everyone also speaks English and Spanish.

LODGING

VILLA RENTALS➤ **Villas International** (⊠ 605 Market St., San Francisco, CA 94105, ☎ 415/281–0910 or 800/221–2260, FAX 415/281–0919).

MAIL

Telegrams and telexes can be sent through SETAR, at the Post Office Building in Oranjestad, or via your hotel. There is also a SETAR office in the new Royal Plaza Mall and in front of the Hyatt Regency Hotel, adjacent to the hotel's parking lot (☎ 297/8–67138).

You can send an airmail letter from Aruba to the United States and Canada for AFl1.40, or US80¢, for the first 10 grams, and a postcard for AFl.60, or US35¢; a letter and postcard to Europe costs AFl1.50 and AFl.70 respectively (US90¢ and US40¢).

MONEY

Arubans happily accept U.S. dollars everywhere, so there's no real need to exchange money, except for necessary pocket change (for soda machines or pay phones). Be aware that shops and restaurants will have difficulty changing US$100 bills. The actual currency is the Aruban florin (AFl), which at press time exchanged to the U.S. dollar at AFl1.77 for cash, AFl1.79 for traveler's checks, and to the Canadian dollar at AFl1.51. The Dutch Antillean florin (used in Bonaire and Curaçao) is not accepted in Aruba. If you need fast cash, you'll find international ATMs that accept international cards at the major malls, Caribbean Mercantile Bank, and Amro Bank. Major credit cards and traveler's checks are widely accepted (with ID). Prices quoted in this guide are in U.S. dollars unless otherwise noted.

ATMS

Before leaving home, **make sure that your credit cards have been programmed for ATM use in Aruba.** Note that Discover is accepted mostly in the United States. Local bank cards often do not work overseas or may access only your checking account; **ask your bank about a MasterCard/Cirrus or Visa debit card,** which works like a bank card but can be used at any ATM displaying a MasterCard/Cirrus or Visa logo. These cards, too, may tap only your checking account; check with your bank about their policy.

A list of Plus locations is available at your local bank. Locations of Cirrus ATMs at press time include the airport, Noord 23A, Pueblo Food Center, L. G. Smith Blvd. 108, Caya Betico Croes 41, Zeppenveldstraat 38 in San Nicholas, and Savaneta 90.

CURRENCY EXCHANGE

For the most favorable rates, **change money at banks.** Although fees charged for ATM transactions may be higher abroad than at home, Cirrus and Plus exchange rates are excellent because they are based on wholesale rates offered only by major banks. You won't do as well at exchange booths in airports or rail and bus stations, in hotels, in restaurants, or in stores, although you may find their hours more convenient. To avoid lines at airport exchange booths, **get a small amount of local currency before you leave home.**

EXCHANGE SERVICES➤ **International Currency Express** (☎ 888/842–0880 on the East Coast or 888/278–6628 on the West Coast for telephone orders). **Thomas Cook Currency Services** (☎ 800/287–7362 for telephone orders and retail locations).

TRAVELER'S CHECKS

Whether or not to buy traveler's checks depends on where you are headed. **Take cash if your trip includes rural areas** and small towns, traveler's checks to cities. If your checks are lost or stolen, they can usually be replaced within 24 hours. To ensure a speedy refund, buy your checks yourself (don't ask someone else to make the purchase). When making a claim for stolen or lost checks, the person who bought the checks should make the call.

PASSPORTS & VISAS

U.S. and Canadian residents need only show proof of identity—a valid passport, a birth certificate with a raised seal together with a photo ID (a driver's license will do), naturalization certificate, green card, valid nonquota immigration visa, or valid voter registration card. All other nationalities must submit a valid passport. Everyone must also possess a return-trip ticket to their country of origin or elsewhere.

Non-U.S. citizens residing in the United States and Canadians residing in the United States or Canada should have a re-entry permit, a valid non-quota immigration visa or an Alien Registration (green card).

Once your travel plans are confirmed, **check the expiration date of your passport.** It's also a good idea to **make photocopies of the data page**; leave one copy with someone at home and keep another with you, separated from your passport. If you lose your passport, promptly call the nearest embassy or consulate and the local police; having a copy of the data page can speed replacement.

U.S. INFORMATION➤ **Office of Passport Services** (☎ 202/647–0518).

CANADA INFORMATION➤ **Passport Office** (☎ 819/994–3500 or 800/567–6868).

U.K. INFORMATION➤ **London Passport Office** (☎ 0990/21010) for fees and documentation requirements and to request an emergency passport.

PRECAUTIONS

Aruba is a relatively safe island, but common-sense rules still apply. Don't leave things in a rental car, and lock the car when you leave it. Leave valuables in your hotel safe, and don't leave bags unattended in the airport, on the beach, or on tour transports. Arubans are very friendly, so you needn't be afraid to stop and ask anyone for directions.

International traffic signs and Dutch-style traffic signals (with an extra light for the turning lane) can be misleading for some American drivers, so use extreme caution—especially at intersections—until you grasp the rules of the road.

Mosquitoes can be bothersome during the rainy season (November through March), so **pack some insect repellent.** The strong trade winds are a relief in the subtropical climate, but don't hang your bathing suit on a balcony—it will probably blow away. Help Arubans conserve water and energy: Turn off air-conditioning when you leave your room and keep your faucets turned off.

TAXES & SERVICE CHARGES

Hotels collect a 6% government tax and usually add an 11% service charge to room bills. You will sometimes see a $3-per-day energy surcharge tacked on to the hotel bill. Restaurants usually add a 10%–15% service charge to your bill. The departure tax is $20 if your airline hasn't already included the tax into your airfare. An ABB tax (a value-added tax) was initiated in mid-1996, and you'll pay it in all but duty-free shops. Taxi drivers are tipped 10% and porters an average of US50¢ per bag.

TAXIS

There is a dispatch office at the airport and behind the Eagle Bowling Palace on Sasaki Road (☎ 297/8–22116); you can also flag down taxis on the street. Taxis do not have meters, and rates are fixed according to districts, so **confirm information before the ride begins.** Fares are for a maximum of four passengers; add $1 to the fare after midnight and on holidays. All Aruba taxi drivers have participated in the government's Tourism Awareness programs and have received a Tourism Guide Certificate. An hour's tour of the island by taxi will run you about $25 for a maximum of four people per car. A taxi from the airport to most hotels will run $12–$17.

TELEPHONES

To dial direct to Aruba from the United States, dial 011–297–8 followed by the five-digit number in Aruba (the area code was recently changed from 809). Local and international calls from Aruba can be made via hotel operators or from the Government Long Distance Telephone, Telegraph, and Radio Office, SETAR, in the Post Office Building in Oranjestad. When dialing locally in Aruba, simply dial the five-digit number. To reach the United States, dial 001, then the area code and number. Local calls from a pay phone cost AFl.25.

CALLING HOME

Before you go, **find out the local access codes** for your destinations. AT&T, MCI, and Sprint long-distance services make calling home relatively convenient, but you may find the local access number blocked in many hotel rooms. First ask the hotel operator to connect you. If the hotel operator balks, ask for an international operator or dial the international operator yourself. One way to improve your odds of getting connected to your long-distance carrier is to **travel with more than one company's calling card** (a hotel may block Sprint, for example, but not MCI). If all else fails, call your phone company collect in the United States or call from a pay phone in the hotel lobby.

To Obtain Access Codes➤ **AT&T USADirect** (☎ 800/874–4000). **MCI Call USA** (☎ 800/444–4444). **Sprint Express** (☎ 800/793–1153).

TOUR OPERATORS

Buying a prepackaged tour or independent vacation can make your trip to Aruba less expensive and more hassle-free. Because everything is prearranged, you'll spend less time planning.

Operators that handle several hundred thousand travelers per year can use their purchasing power to give you a good price. Their high volume may also indicate financial stability. But some small companies provide more personalized service; because they tend to specialize, they may also be more knowledgeable about a given area.

A GOOD DEAL?

The more your package or tour includes, the better you can predict the ultimate cost of your vacation. Make sure you know exactly what is covered, and **beware of hidden costs.** Are taxes, tips, and service charges included? Transfers and baggage handling? Entertainment and excursions? These can add up.

If the package or tour you are considering is priced lower than in your wildest dreams, **be skeptical.** Also, **make sure your travel agent knows the accommodations** and other services. Ask about the hotel's location, room size, beds, and whether it has a pool, room service, and programs for children, if you care about these. Has your agent been there in person or sent others you can contact?

BUYER BEWARE

Each year consumers are stranded or lose their money when tour operators—even very large ones with excellent reputations—go out of

business. So **check out the operator.** Find out how long the company has been in business, and ask several agents about its reputation. **Don't book unless the firm has a consumer-protection program.**

Members of the National Tour Association and United States Tour Operators Association are required to set aside funds to cover your payments and travel arrangements in case the company defaults. Nonmembers may carry insurance instead. Look for the details, and for the name of an underwriter with a solid reputation, in the operator's brochure. Note: When it comes to tour operators, **don't trust escrow accounts.** Although the Department of Transportation watches over charter-flight operators, no regulatory body prevents tour operators from raiding the till. You may want to protect yourself by buying travel insurance that includes a tour-operator default provision.

It's also a good idea to choose a company that participates in the American Society of Travel Agents' Tour Operator Program (TOP). This gives you a forum if there are any disputes between you and your tour operator; ASTA will act as mediator.

TOUR-OPERATOR RECOMMENDATIONS➤ **American Society of Travel Agents** (☞ Travel Agencies, *below*). **National Tour Association** (NTA; ⊠ 546 E. Main St.,

Lexington, KY 40508, ☎ 606/226–4444 or 800/755–8687). **United States Tour Operators Association** (USTOA; ✉ 342 Madison Ave., Suite 1522, New York, NY 10173, ☎ 212/599–6599, ℻ 212/599–6744).

USING AN AGENT

Travel agents are excellent resources. In fact, large operators accept bookings made only through travel agents. But it's a good idea to **collect brochures from several agencies,** because some agents' suggestions may be influenced by relationships with tour and package firms that reward them for volume sales. If you have a special interest, **find an agent with expertise in that area;** ASTA (☞ Travel Agencies, *below*) has a database of specialists worldwide. Do some homework on your own, too: Local tourism boards can provide information about lesser-known and small-niche operators, some of which may sell only direct.

SINGLE TRAVELERS

Prices for packages and tours are usually quoted per person, based on two sharing a room. If traveling solo, you may be required to pay the full double-occupancy rate. Some operators eliminate this surcharge if you agree to be matched with a roommate of the same sex, even if one is not found by departure time.

GUIDED TOURS

For orientation, boat, and special-interest tour operators, *see* Guided Tours at the end of Chapter 7.

PACKAGES

Like group tours, independent vacation packages are available from major tour operators and airlines. The companies listed below offer vacation packages in a broad price range.

Air/Hotel➤ **American Airlines Fly AAway Vacations** (☎ 800/321–2121). **Certified Vacations** (✉ 110 E. Broward Blvd., Fort Lauderdale, FL 33302, ☎ 954/522–1440 or 800/233–7260). **Delta Dream Vacations** (☎ 800/872–7786, ℻ 954/357–4687).

TRAVEL AGENCIES

A good travel agent puts your needs first. Look for an agency that has been in business at least five years, emphasizes customer service, and has someone on staff who specializes in your destination. In addition, **make sure the agency belongs to the American Society of Travel Agents** (ASTA). If your travel agency is also acting as your tour operator, *see* Tour Operators, *above*.

Agency Referrals➤ **American Society of Travel Agents** (ASTA; ☎ 800/965–2782 for 24-hr hot line, ℻ 703/684–8319). **Alliance of Canadian Travel Associations** (✉ 1729 Bank St., Suite 201,

Ottawa, Ontario K1V 7Z5, ☎ 613/521–0474, FAX 613/521–0805). **Association of British Travel Agents** (✉ 55–57 Newman St., London W1P 4AH, ☎ 0171/637–2444, FAX 0171/637–0713).

VISITOR INFORMATION

The Aruba Tourism Authority can be a good source of general information, up-to-date calendars of events, and listings of hotels, restaurants, sights, and shops.

IN THE U.S.➣ **Aruba Tourism Authority** (☎ 800/862–7822). In Florida (✉ 1 Financial Plaza, Suite 136, Fort Lauderdale 33394, ☎ 954/767–2720, FAX 954/767–0432); in Georgia (✉ 199 14th St. NE, Suite 2008, Atlanta 30309-3688, ☎ 404/892–7822, FAX 404/873–2913); in New Jersey (✉ 1000 Harbor Blvd., Ground Level, Weehawken 07087, ☎ 201/330–0800, FAX 201/330–8757); in Texas (✉ 12707 North Freeway, Suite 138, Houston 77060-1234, ☎ 713/872–7822, FAX 713/872–7872).

IN CANADA➣ **Aruba Tourism Authority** (✉ 86 Bloor St. W, Suite 204, Toronto, Ontario, M5S 1M5, ☎ 416/975–1950 or 800/268–3042).

IN EUROPE➣ **Aruba Tourism Authority** (✉ Schimmelpennincklaan 1, 2517 JN, The Hague, The Netherlands, ☎ 70–356–6220, FAX 70–360–4877).

IN ARUBA➣ **Aruba Tourism Authority** (✉ L. G. Smith Blvd. 172, Eagle Beach, Aruba, ☎ 297/8–23777, FAX 297/8–34702), with free brochures and information officers ready to answer questions.

WHEN TO GO

The Aruban climate is fairly constant year-round, with an average temperature of 83°F (27°C). (Because hotel and restaurant air-conditioning can be frigid, bring a light sweater.)

Aruba receives just about 17 inches of rain a year and lies well outside the hurricane belt, so **don't worry about the fall hurricane season** affecting your stay.

Aruba's high season runs from mid-December through mid-April. Carnival revelers make January through March the most expensive and crowded time, so come in the low season between mid-April and September if you're looking for lower rates and a quieter atmosphere.

1 Destination: Aruba

FUN ON A DESERT ISLAND

IMAGINE ARUBA** as one big *Love Boat* cruise. Most of its 29 hotels sit side by side down one major strip along the southwestern shore, with restaurants, exotic boutiques, fiery floor shows, and glitzy casinos right on their premises. Nearly every night there are organized theme parties, treasure hunts, beachside barbecues, and fish fries with steel bands and limbo or Carnival dancers. Surround all this with warm blue-green waters that afford clear visibility up to 100 ft, and you've got the perfect sun destination for travelers seeking entertainment and activities.

Nineteen miles north of Venezuela and the vast South American continent, Aruba is small—only 19½ mi long and 6 mi across at its widest point. Once a member of the Netherlands Antilles, Aruba became an independent entity within the Netherlands in 1986, with its own royally appointed governor, a democratic government, and a 21-member elected Parliament. With education, housing, and health care financed by an economy based on tourism, the island's population of 84,500 recognizes visitors as valued guests. The national anthem proclaims, "The greatness of our people is

their great cordiality," and this is no exaggeration. Waiters serve you with smiles, English is spoken everywhere, and hotel hospitality directors appear delighted to serve your special needs. The result is that Aruba enjoys one of the highest rates of repeat visitors in the Caribbean. Direct air service from the United States makes Aruba an excellent choice for even short vacations.

The island's distinctive beauty lies in its countryside—an almost extraterrestrial landscape full of rocky deserts, divi-divi trees, cactus jungles alive with the chittering of wild parakeets, secluded coves, and aquamarine vistas with crashing waves. With its low humidity and average temperature of 83°F (27°C), Aruba has the climate of a paradise (rain comes mostly during November). Sun, cooling trade winds, friendly and courteous service, modern and efficient amenities, golf and tennis clubs, modern casinos, glorious beaches, duty-free shopping, and some of the best cuisine in the Caribbean (the island swept the Caribbean Culinary Competition in late 1996) make up Aruba's strong suit and help fill its more than 7,000 hotel rooms.

PLEASURES AND PASTIMES

Beaches

All of Aruba's hotels are on the leeward side of the island, but their beaches still catch the constant breezes and gentle surf that make watersports all the more fun. By car, you can discover isolated coves with still waters. The rough waters of the island's windward side are perfect for those who just want to daydream to the crash of the waves.

Cuisine

Aruba has some of the best quality and most diverse restaurants in the Caribbean. Well-stocked kitchens create imaginative menus with fresh and frequent imports from nearby South America. In 1996 the Aruba team of chefs captured the gold medal at the Caribbean Culinary Competition. In addition to gourmet entrées, try the fresh, local seafood dishes. Many hotel restaurants will even cook your own catch for you.

Gambling

The number of casinos on Aruba is up to eleven, as gambling continues to be a favorite island indulgence. It may be scary to think of it as a 1,001 different ways to part with your hard-earned vacation dollars, but once you know your way around the casino, you may find trying your hand quite a thrill. Our Gambling Primer will help build your knowledge and confidence—just don't bet the house.

Windsurfing

Besides keeping landlubbers cool, steady winds make Aruba one of the premier windsurfing spots in the world; windsurfing is also one of the fastest growing sports. Although it may seem that physical strength is the key, a relaxed and balanced approach to "reading the wind" is more important. Lessons are easily arranged at most hotels, and there are beaches and surfs for every skill level.

FESTIVALS AND SEASONAL EVENTS

Aruba's **Carnival** is the most exuberant time of the year; it begins in mid-January and ends in mid-February. A month of parties and parades of colorful costumes, steel and brass bands, dances, and floats culminate in the Grand Carnival parade, held on the Sunday before Ash Wednesday. The parade starts in the late morning in Oranjestad and continues throughout the streets into the evening. Book your hotel far in advance if you plan on partaking in the fun.

At the end of June, the **Aruba Jazz and Latin Music Festival,** in Oranjestad, presents international entertainers performing Latin, pop, jazz, and salsa music at Mansur Stadium. Performers have included

George Benson, Hiroshima, Roberta Flack, Kenny G, Celia Cruz, Tito Puente, Diane Schuur, Al Jarreau, and Carlos Santana.

The **Catamaran Regatta** takes place over a week in November, when catamarans compete in front of the high-rise hotels on the Palm Beach strip.

The year-round **Bon-Bini Festival** of music, crafts, food, and folkloric shows takes place every Tuesday evening from 6:30 to 8:30 at Fort Zoutman in Oranjestad.

Official holidays include January 25, in memory of G. F. Croes, the political leader who attained "Status Aparte" from Holland; March 18, National Anthem and Flag Day, when musical and folkloric events take place at the Plaza Betico Croes; Queen's Day, on April 30, in honor of Queen Beatrix of the Netherlands; and Labor Day, on May 1.

Aruba

California Pt.

California Sand Dunes

Malmok Beach

Mt. Alto Vista

Fisherman's Hut
Palm Beach

Bushiribana ○

○Andico

○ Noord

○ Paradera

Eagle Beach

Manchebo Beach
Divi Beach
Druif Bay

Oranjestad ○

Santa Cruz ○

Queen Beatrix International Airport

Balashi ○

Spanish Lagoon

N

0		4 miles
0		6 km

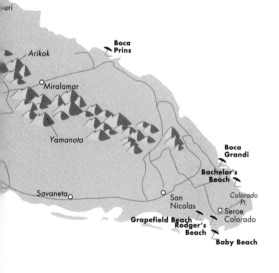

Caribbean Sea

uri

Boca
Prins

Arikok

○Miralamar

Yamanota

Boca
Grandi

Bachelor's
Beach

Savaneta○

○San
Nicolas

*Colorado
Pt.*

○Seroe
Colorado

Grapefield Beach
Rodger's
Beach

Baby Beach

2 Lodging

MOST HOTELS ARE WEST of Oranjestad along L. G. Smith and J. E. Irausquin boulevards and are miniresort complexes, with—get ready—their own drugstores, boutiques, fitness centers, beauty parlors, casinos, restaurants, gourmet delis, water-sports centers, and car-rental and travel desks. Meeting rooms, room service, laundry and dry cleaning services, in-room safe and minibar or refrigerator, and baby-sitting are standard amenities at all but the smallest properties, and daily activities (beach bingo or volleyball, aquacise or aerobics, crafts classes, even Papiamento dialect lessons, and separate supervised activities for children) are usually part of the package. Children often get free accommodation in their parents' room; check with the property for age qualifications. Hotel restaurants and clubs are open to all guests on the island, so you can visit other properties no matter where you're staying. Most hotels, unless specified, do not include meals in their room rates.

To save money (hotels are fairly expensive in Aruba), take advantage of the many airline and hotel packages, which are plentiful and considerably less expensive than the one-night rate. Or go during low season (summer), when rates are discounted up to 40%.

CATEGORY	COST*
$$$$	over $300
$$$	$225–$300
$$	$150–$225
$	under $150

All prices are for a standard double room during high season, excluding 6% government tax and 11% service charge.

$$$$ ☷ **Americana Aruba Beach Resort & Casino.** Teeming activity surrounds the clover-leaf-shape pool with a waterfall and two whirlpool tubs at the heart of this large resort. The buzz is indicative of the atmosphere in general: A social director is always cajoling you to participate in everything from beer-drinking contests to bikini shows. The property recently underwent a $3.5 million face-lift, and rooms are now done in richer shades of purple, green, and yellow and furnished in light rattan. Still, this one is just not as luxu-

rious as others in its price range. White-tiled bathrooms are a bit tight, and balconies are no more than narrow step-outs. However, it remains popular with American and Canadian tour groups. ⊠ *J. E. Irausquin Blvd. 83, Palm Beach,* ☎ *297/8–24500 or 800/447–7462,* FAX *297/8–23191. 419 rooms. 2 restaurants, 4 bars, pool, 2 outdoor hot tubs, 2 tennis courts, exercise room, Ping-Pong, volleyball, beach, water sports, casino. AE, D, DC, MC, V. EP, All-inclusive.*

$$$$ 🏨 **Aruba Marriott Resort and Stellaris Casino.** Aruba's newest (1995)—and most expensive—luxury high-rise resort opened on the far end of Palm Beach close to the Tierra del Sol Golf Course. You'll hear the sound of water everywhere, whether it's the trickling of streams and waterfalls in the elegant marble lobby and around the tropically landscaped free-form pool or the beating of the surf. The rooms are spacious and attractively appointed (crisp, clean forest-green-on-white decor softened by floral bedspreads and pastel watercolor paintings), and all have an ocean view and a balcony. The hotel's pricey gourmet restaurant, Tuscanny's, has developed a strong reputation in a short amount of time. ⊠ *L. G. Smith Blvd. 101, Palm Beach,* ☎ *297/8–69000 or 800/223–6388,* FAX *297/8–60649. 413 rooms, 18 suites. 3 restaurants, 5 bars, café, no-smoking floors, pool, indoor and outdoor hot tubs, massage, saunas, spa, 3 tennis courts, aerobics, health club, horseshoes, volleyball, water sports, scuba diving, shops, casino, concierge. AE, D, DC, MC, V. EP, MAP, FAP, All-inclusive.*

$$$$ 🏨 **Hyatt Regency Aruba Resort & Casino.** This $57 million
★ resort, a favorite among Aruba's luxury properties, looks like a Spanish grandee's palace, with Art Deco–style flourishes and a multilevel pool with waterfalls, a two-story water slide, and a lagoon stocked with tropical fish and black swans. Rooms, done in gemstone color schemes and dark mahogany furnishings, have tiny step-out balconies and a lot of little extras. Four excellent restaurants are on the premises, among them Olé and Ruinas del Mar. Their design is exquisite: stone-and-marble "ruins" surrounded by moats, waterfalls, and splashing fountains. It is a truly romantic resort, with lush grounds perfect for an evening

stroll—a top choice for honeymooners. ✉ *J. E. Irausquin Blvd. 85, Palm Beach,* ☎ *297/8–61234 or 800/233–1234,* FAX *297/8–61682. 342 rooms, 18 suites. 4 restaurants, 5 bars, snack bar, no-smoking floor, room service, pool, beauty salon, 2 outdoor hot tubs, massage, sauna, steam rooms, 2 tennis courts, health club, volleyball, beach, dive shop, dock, water sports, fishing, shops, casino, playground. AE, DC, MC, V. EP, MAP.*

$$$–$$$$ 🏨 **Sonesta Resorts at Seaport Village.** For those who enjoy
★ being in the thick of things, this sprawling property downtown is surrounded by shops, restaurants, and casinos galore. The resort includes two hotels: the newer one, with roomy suites set near a small man-made beach, and the original high-rise, with compact but attractive rooms above the Seaport Mall (pick the quieter garden-view rooms here). In the resort lobby, which connects to the mall, parrots fly free in the tropical garden atrium and guests board motor skiffs headed for the resort's 40-acre private island—perfect for day trips. The gourmet restaurant, L'Escale, is one of Aruba's most creative—and expensive. This lively property is a top choice for singles and offers plenty for families, too. ✉ *L. G. Smith Blvd. 9, Oranjestad,* ☎ *297/8–36000 or 800/766–3782,* FAX *297/8–34389. Sonesta Resort & Casino: 285 rooms, 15 suites; Sonesta Suites & Casino: 250 suites. 4 restaurants, 4 bars, kitchenettes, no-smoking floor, 2 pools, massage, tennis court, aerobics, exercise room, volleyball, beach, shops, 2 casinos, nightclub, playground, coin laundry, concierge, convention center. AE, DC, MC, V. EP, MAP, FAP, All-inclusive.*

$$$ 🏨 **Wyndham Aruba Beach Resort and Casino.** The grand public areas of the Wyndham are dazzling in size and scope and cavernous enough to accommodate conventioneers and big groups, which make up a good portion of the resort's clientele. If bustle and nonstop activity make your day, you'll be right at home here. Rooms, average in size, are pretty in dusty rose, peach, and sea-foam green and thoughtfully equipped with coffeemaker, iron and ironing board, refrigerator, hair dryer, and ocean-view balcony. Fountains splash playfully into the 8,000-square-ft free-form pool, and the Casablanca Casino has Rick's Place in mind. A full-service spa, with all the muds and rubs, an extensive

Aruba Lodging

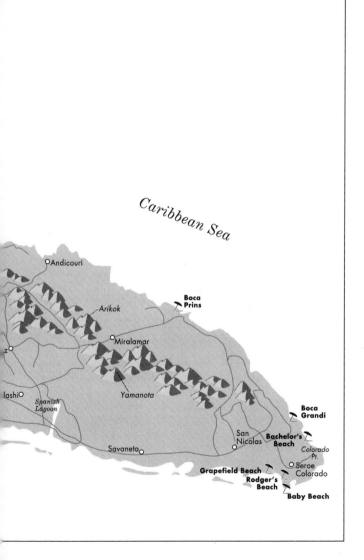

Caribbean Sea

Andicouri

Arikok

Boca
Prins

Miralamar

Yamanota

z

Iashi

Spanish
Lagoon

Boca
Grandi

San
Nicolas

Bachelor's
Beach

Savaneta

Colorado
Pt.

Grapefield Beach

Seroe
Colorado

Rodger's
Beach

Baby Beach

program of day and night activities for the kids, and the Red Sail water-sports facility on the beach are pluses. There is a fee for use of the health club. ⊠ *J. E. Irausquin Blvd. 77, Palm Beach,* ☎ *297/8–64466 or 800/996–3426,* 𝔽𝔸𝕏 *297/8–68217. 378 rooms, 66 suites. 4 restaurants, 4 bars, deli, pool, wading pool, beauty salon, massage, sauna, steam room, tennis court, health club, Ping-Pong, shuffle-board, volleyball, beach, dive shop, water sports, shops, casino, playground, concierge, convention center. AE, DC, MC, V. EP, CP, MAP, FAP.*

$$–$$$ 🏨 **Holiday Inn Aruba Beach Resort & Casino.** This is one of the larger properties on Palm Beach, but its size is cleverly camouflaged. Three buildings of seven stories each are set apart from each other along a sugary-looking, palm-dotted beach. Rooms, redone during resort-wide renovations in 1996, are clean, spacious, and attractive in shades of pale green and rose. The pool was also redone, and its cascading waterfalls and sunning deck draw as large a crowd as the wide beach, perhaps because this area is the site of organized activities for adults and children. This friendly, reasonably priced resort is a reliable choice for families. ⊠ *J. E. Irausquin Blvd. 230, Palm Beach,* ☎ *297/8–63600 or 800/465–4329,* 𝔽𝔸𝕏 *297/8–65165. 600 rooms. 3 restaurants, 3 bars, no-smoking rooms, refrigerators, pool, massage, 6 tennis courts, boccie, exercise room, Ping-Pong, beach, dock, dive shop, water sports, shops, casino, concierge. AE, DC, MC, V. EP, MAP, FAP.*

$$–$$$ 🏨 **Mill Resort.** Two-story red-roof buildings flank the open-air common areas of this small condominium hotel. Request one of the rooms renovated in 1996; they are far more attractive and modern, with a pastel tropical decor. The junior suites have a king-size bed, a sitting area, and fully equipped kitchenette. Studios have a full kitchen but only a queen-size convertible sofa bed, a tiny bathroom, and no balcony. This moderately priced resort is popular with couples seeking a quiet getaway and with families with small children. To the relief of many guests, there are no casino and no organized evening activities; action can be found at the nearby large resorts, and the beach is only a five-minute walk (though there is a beach shuttle). At press time, there was talk of adding another 200 rooms and taking over management of the neighboring Old Mill restaurant (☞ Chapter 3). ⊠ *J. E. Irausquin Blvd. 330, Noord, ☎ 297/8–67700, FAX 297/8–67271. 200 rooms. Bar, grill, grocery, kitchenette, pool, wading pool, saunas, 2 tennis courts, exercise room, coin laundry. AE, DC, MC, V. EP.*

$$–$$$ 🏨 **Radisson Aruba Caribbean Resort & Casino.** Called La Grande Dame of the Caribbean, this resort was the first highrise on the island. Liz Taylor used to stay here when she was married to Eddie Fisher, so the outgoing staff is used to filling special needs. The broad beach dotted by shade huts is the site of many of the resort's organized activities. A comprehensive renewal has brought flowers, artwork, and a generally festive air to the lobby. Of the sunny air-conditioned rooms with balconies, 65% have a full ocean view. Larger TVs, bamboo furniture, and tropical-print bedspreads and curtains are among the welcome recent additions. ⊠ *J. E. Irausquin Blvd. 81, Palm Beach, ☎ 297/8–66555 or 800/333–3333, FAX 297/8–63260. 353 rooms, 19 suites. 3 restaurants, 4 bars, café, ice cream parlor, no-smoking rooms, pool, 4 tennis courts, basketball, boccie, exercise room, shuffleboard, volleyball, beach, dive shop, water sports, shops, casino, library, playground. AE, D, DC, MC, V. EP, MAP, FAP.*

$$ 🏨 **Bucuti Beach Resort.** The intimate, European-style Bu-
★ cuti Beach is a refreshingly peaceful antidote to the impersonal feel of some larger, bustling resorts. From the moment you are seated and handed a refreshing cool towel in the new lobby, it's clear that the gracious staff has an understanding of the art of hospitality. Hacienda-style buildings house enormous rooms with bright floral decor, sparkling tile floors, and terrace or balcony with ocean view. In-room extras include hair dryers, minibar, microwave, iron, ironing board, and coffeemakers. The resort has an enviable beach location, on the widest, most secluded section of Eagle Beach. The breezy oceanfront Pirate's Nest restaurant, which looks like a beached galleon, is known island-wide for its excellent theme dinners. ⊠ *J. E. Irausquin Blvd. 55-B, Eagle Beach, ☎ 297/8–36141 or 800/528–1234, FAX 297/8–25272. 63 rooms. Restaurant, bar, pool, exercise room, volleyball, beach, bicycles, shop. AE, D, DC, MC, V. CP, MAP.*

\$\$ ⊞ **Divi Aruba Beach Resort.** The motto at this popular Mediterranean-style low rise remains "barefoot elegance," which means you can streak through the lobby in your bikini. The main section of the resort has standard guest rooms, beachfront lanai rooms, and casitas (garden bungalows) that look out onto individual courtyards and for the most part are only steps away from the beach. The guest rooms are on the island's water system, which means the water is cooled and heated by Mother Nature—just another reason to wish for warm weather. Remodeled bathrooms, white-tile floors, updated light-wood furniture, and fresh paint have helped tremendously. There is a daily activities program and theme dinners each night; the Red Parrot restaurant offers romantic beachside dining. ⊠ *L. G. Smith Blvd. 93, Divi Beach, Oranjestad,* ☎ *297/8–23300 or 800/554–2008,* 𝖥𝖠𝖷 *297/8–31940. 203 rooms. 2 restaurants, 2 bars, refrigerators, 2 pools, outdoor hot tub, tennis court, shuffleboard, volleyball, beach, dive shop, water sports, mountain bikes, shops. AE, D, DC, MC, V. EP, MAP, FAP, All-inclusive.*

\$\$ ⊞ **La Cabana All Suite Beach Resort & Casino.** At the top end of Eagle Beach, across the busy road from the sand, is Aruba's largest time-sharing complex. The original four-story building faces the beach and forms a horseshoe around a huge free-form pool complex, with a water slide, a poolside bar, an outdoor café, and a water-sports center. One-third of the rooms have a full sea view. All the oddly configured but comfortable rooms—studio suites or one-bedroom suites—come with a fully equipped kitchenette, a small balcony, and a whirlpool bath for two. Pricier suites and villas are separated from the main building by a parking lot, making them more secluded and quieter. Shuttle buses run guests over to the upscale casino, where the hotel has a theme restaurant and the Tropicana showroom. ⊠ *J. E. Irausquin Blvd. 250, Eagle Beach,* ☎ *297/8– 39000 or 800/835–7193; 212/251–1710 in NY;* 𝖥𝖠𝖷 *297/8–37208. 803 suites. 4 restaurants, 3 bars, ice cream parlor, grocery, 3 pools, 3 outdoor hot tubs, massage, sauna, aerobics, basketball, health club, racquetball, shuffleboard, squash, volleyball, beach, dive shop, water sports, shops, casino, theater, playground, coin laundry, chapel. AE, DC, MC, V. EP, MAP, FAP, All-inclusive.*

$–$$ ⊞ **Amsterdam Manor Beach Resort.** This attractive gabled, mustard-color hotel looks like part of a Dutch colonial village. Rooms are furnished either in Dutch modern or provincial style and range from smallish studios with a balcony and a whirlpool bathtub to deluxe two-bedroom suites with peaked ceilings, a whirlpool bathtub and shower, and a full kitchen. It's a cozy enclave surrounding a lovely pool with waterfall, marred only slightly by the noise of traffic from J. E. Irausquin Boulevard. At least the glorious Eagle Beach is just across the street. Complimentary diving lessons are available twice each week, and there aren't many other planned activities, so the property stays fairly peaceful. ⊠ *J. E. Irausquin Blvd. 252, Eagle Beach,* ☎ *297/8–71492 or 800/766–6016,* ⅏ *297/8–71463. 72 units. Restaurant, bar, pool, snorkeling, playground, coin laundry. AE, MC, V. EP.*

$–$$ ⊞ **Aruba Palm Beach Hotel & Casino.** Dotting the drive leading to this pink eight-story Moorish palazzo are pink-swaddled palm trees. Around the other side is a large, well-manicured tropical garden good for sunning, with a pair of vociferous parrots guarding the entrance. The oversize guest rooms are cheerfully decorated in plaids and tropical prints; each has a large walk-in closet and a postage-stamp balcony that overlooks the ocean, the pool, or the gardens. An organized activities program keeps things hopping here. For a peaceful meal, eat alfresco in the rock-garden setting of the Seawatch Restaurant. For live music, try the Players Club lounge. A limbo and steelband show is scheduled one night a week. ⊠ *J. E. Irausquin Blvd. 79, Palm Beach,* ☎ *297/8–63900 or 800/345–2782,* ⅏ *297/8–61941. 186 rooms. 2 restaurants, 2 bars, deli, room service, pool, wading pool, 2 tennis courts, volleyball, beach, dive shop, water sports, shops, casino. AE, D, DC, MC, V. EP, MAP.*

$ ⊞ **Aruba Blue Village Suites.** If a plumper wallet is more important to you than a beachfront location, this comfortable enclave tucked away from the hotel strip in a residential area is the answer. The single-story apartments form an open-ended rectangle around one of two pools (where the barbecues are held once a week); each basic but tidy apartment has a fully equipped kitchen, sparse Dutch-style furnishings, and air-conditioned bedrooms. Studios are a fine budget option for a family of four, and there are a playground and a pool area for the little ones. It's 1½ mi to Eagle Beach, but there's shuttle service a few times a day. If you want to go sightseeing or shopping, though, you'll need a car. ⊠ *Cunucu Abao 37, Oranjestad,* ☎ *297/8–78618 or 800/338–3108,* FAX *297/8–70081. 56 studios, 1- and 2-bedroom suites. 2 pools, sauna, exercise room, Ping-Pong, playground. AE, DC, MC, V. EP.*

$ **⊞ Bushiri Beach Resort.** Two long, low buildings—built around three hot tubs surrounded by lush foliage and situated on a wide expanse of beach—make up Aruba's first all-inclusive resort. These buildings are old and nondescript, and although the rooms were renovated, they remain fairly plain. But the Bushiri is a hotel-training school, a factor that shows in the enthusiastic staff. Where this resort shines is in its full daily activities program for adults and supervised program for kids. Island tours and casino trips, three meals a day, a poolside barbecue, a midnight buffet, and all beverages are part of the package—considering all that's included, it's quite a bargain. ⊠ *L. G. Smith Blvd. 35, Oranjestad,* ☎ *297/8–25216, 800/462–6867, or 800/462–6868;* FAX *297/8–26789. 150 rooms, 4 suites. Restaurant, 2 bars, grill, refrigerators, pool, wading pool, beauty salon, 3 outdoor hot tubs, 2 tennis courts, exercise room, Ping-Pong, beach, water sports, boating, fishing, airport shuttle. AE, DC, MC, V. All-inclusive.*

$ **⊞ Coconut Inn.** It's best to have a car if you're staying at this budget hotel, a five-minute drive inland from hotel row on Palm Beach. Request one of the "deluxe studios" in the two-story white building and accept no substitute (the rest of the rooms are old, musty, dark, and lacking in cheer). These new rooms have a microwave and a refrigerator; strong, quiet air-conditioners; white-tile floors and bathrooms; modern furnishings; and a small balcony or patio overlooking the rectangular pool. Continental breakfast, included in the $80-a-night tariff, is served in the informal restaurant next to the pool. The public bus stops a short walk away. ⊠ *Angelo Rojer, Noord 31, Noord,* ☎ *297/8–66288,* FAX *297/8–65433. 24 rooms. Restaurant, pool, coin laundry. MC, V. CP.*

$ ⚏ **Stauffer Hotel Aruba.** The four-story Stauffer Hotel offers the best value in accommodations in the high-rise resort zone. Built in 1994 on busy J. E. Irausquin Boulevard across from Palm Beach and the facilities of the Aruba Palm Beach Resort (available for use by the Stauffer guests), there are no grand sea views or sparkling pool here, but $100 per night buys a snug, modern motel-style room in a prime location. There's also a bus stop nearby, so a rental car isn't necessary unless you want to explore the island on your own. ⊠ *J. E. Irausquin Blvd. 370, Palm Beach,* ☎ *297/8–60855,* ℻ *297/8–60856. 100 rooms. Water sports, shop. AE, D, DC, MC, V. EP.*

$ ⚏ **Tamarijn Aruba.** A series of low-rise buildings stretches along the property of this all-inclusive resort on Bravo Beach. The spacious oceanfront rooms have a casual feel, with woven fiber mats on dark tile floors, light rattan and wood furnishings, and patios or balconies. The package here covers meals and snacks, all beverages, nightly entertainment (including theme nights), tickets to the Bon Bini Festival, a sunset cruise, and an array of activities including mountain biking, snorkeling, sailing, and windsurfing (lessons are included as well). It's a low-key, active place, catering primarily to couples and families looking for a bargain. The only price you'll pay is service that could stand some improvement. ⊠ *J. E. Irausquin Blvd. 41, Bravo Beach,* ☎ *297/8–24150 or 800/554–2008,* ℻ *297/8–31940. 236 rooms. 3 restaurants, 4 bars, snack bar, 2 pools, barbershop, 2 tennis courts, Ping-Pong, shuffleboard, volleyball, beach, water sports, fishing, mountain bikes, shops. AE, D, DC, MC, V. All-inclusive.*

$ ⚏ **Vistalmar.** There's no beach here, but the sea is just across the street, along with a swimming pier. Simply furnished air-conditioned one-bedroom apartments have a full kitchen, living room/dining room, and broad sunporch. The friendly owners provide snorkel gear and stock the refrigerator with fixings for breakfast. The drawback at this small complex is its distance from town, but a rental car is included in the rate. ⊠ *A. O. Yarzagaray, Bucutiweg 28, Noord,* ☎ *297/8–28579,* ℻ *297/8–22200. 8 rooms. Coin laundry. No credit cards. CP.*

3 Dining

ARUBA GRABBED THE GOLD at the 1996 Caribbean Culinary Competition, so while you can definitely get something at a fast-food joint, you can also expect to enjoy many outstanding meals during your visit. Most resorts here offer better-than-average hotel dining and several meal plans, which you can purchase either in advance or upon arrival. But before you purchase a Full American Plan (FAP), which includes breakfast, lunch, and dinner, try one of the numerous excellent and reasonably priced restaurants. Restaurants serve a variety of cuisines, although most menus are specifically designed to please American palates—you can get fresh surf and New York turf almost anywhere. It's worth experimenting with Aruban specialties—*pan bati* is a mildly sweet beaten bread that resembles a pancake, plantains are similar to cooked bananas though not as soft or sweet, *scavechi* is marinated fried fish served with polenta-like *funchi,* and *keshi yena* is a marvelous baked concoction of gouda cheese stuffed with spices and meat or seafood in a rich brown sauce.

On Sunday it may be difficult to find a restaurant outside the hotels that's open for lunch, and many restaurants are closed for dinner on Sunday or Monday night. Good hotel options are the extensive buffet at the Holiday Inn or the wonderful champagne brunch at the Hyatt. A 10%–15% service charge is usually added automatically to restaurant bills. Reservations are essential for dinner during high season.

What to Wear

Even the finest restaurants require at the most only a jacket for men and a sundress for women. The air-conditioning does get cold, so don't go bare-armed. And anytime you plan to eat in the open air, remember to first douse yourself from head to toe with insect repellent—the mosquitoes can get unruly.

CATEGORY	COST*
$$$	over $30
$$	$20–$30
$	under $20

*per person for a three-course meal, excluding drinks,
10%–15% service charge, and tax*

$$$ ✕ **Chez Mathilde.** This elegant restaurant occupies one of
★   the last surviving 19th-century houses in Aruba. Ask to sit
     in the swooningly romantic Pavilion Room, which has an
     eclectic mix of turn-of-the-century Italian and French decor,
     ivy-covered walls, and curtained nooks and crannies for pri-
     vacy. Then sit back and enjoy the high culinary standards
     of the French-style menu, which is constantly being re-
     created by the Dutch chef. Feast on artfully presented
     baked escargots with herbs and garlic, bouillabaisse with
     garlic croutons and cream and cognac to taste, grilled
     Canadian salmon with a delicate balsamic dressing, or filet
     mignon in a signature pepper sauce prepared table-side. The
     chef has a deft touch with sauces. Then, too, there are
     crêpes suzette and a chocolate gâteau to tempt the taste buds.
     Reserve a table well in advance. ✉ *Havenstraat 23, Oran-
     jestad,* ☎ *297/8–34968. Reservations essential. AE, DC,
     MC, V. No lunch Sun.*

$$$ ✕ **Papiamento.** Longtime restaurateurs Lenie and Eduardo
★   Ellis decided Aruba needed a bistro that was cozy yet ele-
     gant, intimate, and always romantic. So they converted their
     130-year-old home into just such a spot. Guests can feast
     sumptuously indoors surrounded by antiques or outdoors
     in a patio garden decorated with enormous ceramics (de-
     signed by Lenie) and filled with ficus and palm trees adorned
     with lights. The chef utilizes flavors from both Continen-
     tal and Caribbean cuisines to produce favorites that include
     seafood and meat dishes. Try the Dover sole, the Caribbean
     lobster, shrimp and red snapper cooked table-side on a hot
     marble stone, or the clay pot for two—a medley of seafoods
     prepared in a sealed clay pot. Papiamento has catered to
     Dutch royalty on their state visit. ✉ *Washington 61, Noord,*
     ☎ *297/8–64544. Reservations essential. AE, MC, V. Closed
     Mon. No lunch.*

$$$ ✕ **Valentino's.** The airy two-level dining room is invitingly
     dressed in sparkling white and shades of mint green. The

tables are placed comfortably far apart, and the service is attentive without being overbearing. The Italian menu has knockouts such as the Caribbean lobster on a bed of linguine with marinara sauce. A festive atmosphere makes the restaurant popular with celebrating Arubans. You'll find their gaiety infectious. All this atmosphere means the restaurant is usually booked up days in advance. ⊠ *Caribbean Palm Village, Noord 43E,* ☎ *297/8–62700. Reservations essential. AE, DC, MC, V. Closed Sun. No lunch.*

\$\$ ✕ **Benihana.** Japanese cuisine is fairly new on the dining scene in Aruba, and newest of the Japanese restaurants is this American-based hibachi-grill chain restaurant, conveniently located in the hotel zone. The chefs put on a flashy show of twirling knives as they slice and dice steak, chicken, shrimp, and vegetables at one of 14 cooking tables. Rice, soup, salad, grilled vegetables, and green-tea ice cream (or sherbet) come with the meal. There's also a sushi bar. A Japanese singer croons for guests on weekends. ⊠ *Sasakiweg z/n, Oranjestad,* ☎ *297/8–26788. AE, MC, V.*

\$\$ ✕ **Buccaneer Restaurant.** Imagine you're in a sunken ship— fishnets and turtle shells hang from the ceiling, and through the portholes you see live sharks, barracudas, and groupers swimming by. That's the Buccaneer, a virtual underwater grotto snug in an old stone building flanked by heavy black chains. Add to that a fantastic 5,000-gallon saltwater aquarium plus 12 more porthole-size tanks. The surf-and-turf cuisine is prepared by the chef-owners with European élan. Order the fresh catch of the day or more exotic fare, such as shrimps with Pernod or smoked pork cutlets with sausage, sauerkraut, and potatoes. Go early (around 5:45 PM) to get a booth next to the aquariums. ⊠ *Gasparito 11-C, Noord,* ☎ *297/8–66172. AE, MC, V. Closed Sun. No lunch.*

\$\$ ✕ **Frankie's Prime Grill.** In the splashy new Royal Plaza Mall,
★ Frankie's (owned by the same family that operates the successful Le Petite Café; ☞ *below*) specializes in Argentinian prime beef and grilled seafood. Diners can eat on the palm-filled wraparound terrace or in the more refined, air-conditioned interior of this favorite spot. Prime *churrasco* (a thick slab of beef prepared Argentine-style) and scampi *los*

24

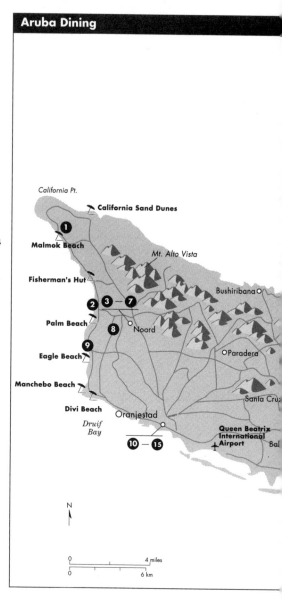

Aruba Dining

California Pt.

California Sand Dunes

Mt. Alto Vista

Malmok Beach

Fisherman's Hut

Bushiribana O

Palm Beach

Noord

O Paradera

Eagle Beach

Manchebo Beach

Santa Cruz

Divi Beach

Oranjestad

Druif Bay

Queen Beatrix International Airport

Bal

N

0   4 miles

0   6 km

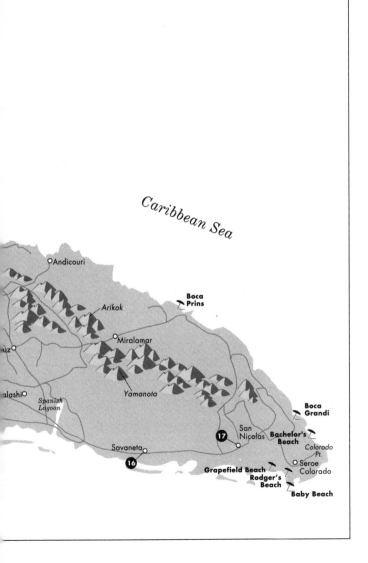

Caribbean Sea

Andicouri

Arikok

Boca
Prins

Miralamar

uz

alashi

Spanish
Lagoon

Yamanota

Boca
Grandi

San
Nicolas

Bachelor's
Beach

17

Savaneta

Colorado
Pt.

Seroe
Colorado

16

Grapefield Beach

Rodger's
Beach

Baby Beach

barquitos (jumbo shrimp sautéed in butter and garlic) are the most popular items. Start with the garlicky escargots, seafood crepe, or Caesar salad (big enough for two), and try to leave room for *tres lechi* (a cool Cuban cake made with three types of milk). ⊠ *Royal Plaza 135, Oranjestad,* ☎ *297/8–38471 or 297/8–38473. AE, DC, MC, V.*

$$ ✕ **Gasparito Restaurant and Art Gallery.** As the name
★ states, this charming restaurant also serves as a gallery, showcasing the works of local artists on softly lighted, creamy white walls. It's set in an authentic *cunucu* (country house) in Noord not far from the hotel strip. The Aruban specialties—pan bati, keshi yena, fish croquettes, conch stew with hot Aruban pepper, stewed chicken, creole-style fish fillet—are also works of art, so it comes as no surprise that Gasparito's chefs walk away with top awards in Caribbean culinary competitions. Service is discreet and very accommodating (they'll stay open if guests come for a late dinner). ⊠ *Gasparito 3, Noord,* ☎ *297/8–67044. AE, D, MC, V. Closed Sun. No lunch.*

$$ ✕ **Old Mill** (De Olde Molen). A gift from the queen of Holland, this real Dutch mill built in 1804 was shipped brick by brick to Aruba in 1920 and reassembled here. For starters, try the seafood crepe Neptune, flamed with Pernod. Also excellent are the beef Stroganoff, Wiener schnitzel, grilled jumbo shrimp, and the Dutch fries—crunchy little nuggets of potato. There are two dinner seatings, at 6:30 and 9. At press time, there was talk of the restaurant's being taken over by the Mill Resort; but with luck, the menu and the focus on quality food will remain the same. ⊠ *J. E. Irausquin Blvd. 330, Noord,* ☎ *297/8–62060. Reservations essential. AE, DC, MC, V. Closed Sun. No lunch.*

$$ ✕ **Ventanas del Mar.** The name means "windows on the sea," which couldn't be more appropriate given the setting above the Tierra del Sol Golf Course at the western tip of the island. This quietly elegant restaurant features floor-to-ceiling windows that look out across the back nine holes and the rolling sand dunes to the sea. Sandwiches, salads, conch fritters, nachos, and quesadillas fill the midday menu; at night the focus is on seafood (roasted red snapper, crab cakes, grilled garlic shrimp, panfried oysters) and meat (prime rib, veal chop in rosemary demiglace, herbed half chicken). ⊠ *Tierra del Sol Golf Course, Malmokweg,* ☎ *297/8–67800. AE, MC, V.*

$–$$ ✕ **Boonoonoonoos.** The name—say it just as it looks!—means "extraordinary," a bit of hyperbole for this Austrian-owned Caribbean bistro in the heart of Oranjestad, but in the fiercely competitive Aruban restaurant business, you gotta have a gimmick. The specialty here is pan-Caribbean cuisine. The decor is simple, but the tasty food, served with hearty portions of peas, rice, and plantains, makes up for the lack of tablecloths, china, and crystal. The roast chicken Barbados is sweet and tangy, marinated in a piña colada sauce. The Jamaican jerk ribs (a 300-year-old recipe) are tiny but spicy, and the satin-smooth hot pumpkin soup drizzled with cheese and served in a pumpkin shell may as well be dessert. Avoid the place when it's crowded, since the service and the quality of the food deteriorate. ⊠ *Wilhelminastraat 18A, Oranjestad,* ☎ *297/8–31888. AE, MC, V. No lunch Sun.*

$–$$ ✕ **Brisas del Mar.** This friendly 16-table place overlooking
★ the sea makes you feel as if you're dining in an Aruban home. Old family recipes use traditional indigenous ingredients like the aromatic *yerbiholé* leaf and the sizzling Mme. Jeanette pepper. Try the smashing steamy fish soup (which would do a Marseillais proud), *keri keri* (shredded fish kissed with annatto seed), or some of the best pan bati on the island. The fresh catch of the day cooked Aruban style (panfried and covered in a tangy creole sauce or panfried in garlic butter on request) has drawn a crowd here for more than 20 years. It's so good it justifies the taxi ride needed to reach it—10 mi east of Oranjestad in the town of Savaneta. ⊠ *Savaneta 222A, Savaneta,* ☎ *297/8–47718. AE, MC, V. No lunch Mon.*

$–$$ ✕ **Old Cunucu House.** On a small estate in a residential neighborhood three minutes from the high-rise hotels, this 75-year-old white-stucco home with slanting roofs, wood beams, and a terra-cotta courtyard filled with bougainvillea has been converted to a laid-back seafood and international cuisine restaurant. Dine on red snapper (or whatever fish happens to be fresh that day), almond-fried shrimp with lobster sauce, Cornish hen, New York sirloin, or beef fondue à deux. An Aruban trio sings and plays background music every Friday, and on Saturday evening a mariachi band serenades the patrons. ⊠ *Palm Beach 150, Noord,* ☎ *297/8–61666. AE, MC, V. Closed Sun. No lunch.*

$ ✕ **Charlie's Restaurant & Bar.** Now an institution, Char-
★   lie's has been a San Nicolas hangout for more than 50 years. During the oil refinery days it was a hopping bar for all kinds of rough-and-scruffs. Now tourists flock here to gawk at the decor: License plates, hard hats, baseball pennants, intimate apparel, and credit cards cover and crowd every inch of the walls and ceiling. House specialties are Argentinian tenderloin and "shrimps—jumbo and dumbo" (dumb because they were caught). You'll have to peel the shell off the shrimp scampi, but needing to wash up afterward gives you a reason to go check out the incredible "decor" in the rest room. And don't leave before trying Charlie's special honeymoon sauce (so called because it's really hot). ⊠ *Zeppenfeldstraat 56, San Nicolas,* ☎ *297/8–45086. No credit cards. Closed Sun.*

$ ✕ **Kowloon.** In addition to many Chinese provinces, Indonesia is also represented on the menu here. Try the *bami goreng,* a noodle-based dish with shreds of shrimp, pork, vegetables, and an Indonesian blend of herbs and spices. *Saté,* curried dishes, and steak prepared in a variety of ways are also available. The modern Asian decor blends easily with the island's palms and sands. ⊠ *Emmastraat 11, Oranjestad,* ☎ *297/8–24950. AE, MC, V.*

$ ✕ **La Paloma.** "The Dove" is a no-frills, low-key Italian eatery tightly packed with tables that are typically overflowing with patrons. Top seller on the international and Italian menu is veal *paisano* (layered veal, mozzarella, ricotta, and spinach baked to bubbling). Caesar salad and minestrone soup are house specialties. This is not the place for a romantic interlude; come for the family atmosphere, simple food, and reasonable prices. ⊠ *Noord 39, Noord,* ☎ *297/8–62770. AE, MC, V. Closed Tues. No lunch.*

$ ✕ **Le Petit Café.** The motto here is "Romancing the stone"— referring to tasty cuisine cooked on hot stones. The low ceiling and hanging plants make this an intimate lunch spot for shoppers. Alfresco dining in the bustling square lets diners keep an eye on things, but fumes from nearby traffic tend to spoil the meal. Jumbo shrimp, sandwiches, ice cream, and fresh fruit dishes are light choices. A second edition of this popular café has opened in the American Hotel. ⊠ *Emmastraat 1, Oranjestad,* ☎ *297/8–26577;* ⊠ *American Hotel, J. E. Irausquin Blvd. 83,* ☎ *297/8–64368. AE, DC, MC, V. No lunch Sun.*

$ ✕ **The Paddock.** This typical Dutch *eet-café* (a café serving full meals) is a casual open-air terrace on the downtown waterfront overlooking the pier and whichever cruise ships happen to be in port. French bread with Brie, fried eggs, bami goreng, saté, and fresh seafood salads are among the lunch and dinner offerings here. All-you-can-eat spareribs ($10) are the focus on Wednesday. There's no automatic service charge added to the bill, so remember to tip the jean-clad waitstaff. ⊠ *L. G. Smith Blvd. 13, Oranjestad,* ☎ *297/8–32334. MC, V.*

4 Beaches, Outdoor Activities, and Sports

BEACHES

BEACHES IN ARUBA are legendary in the Caribbean: white sand, turquoise waters, and virtually no garbage, for everyone takes the no-littering sign—NO TIRA SUSHI—very seriously, especially with an Afl500 fine. The influx of tourists in the past decade, however, has crowded the major beaches, which back up to the hotels along the southwestern strip. These beaches are public, and you can make the two-hour hike from the Holiday Inn to the Bushiri Beach Hotel free of charge and without ever leaving sand. If you go strolling during the day, make sure you are well protected from the sun—it scorches fast, and the trade winds can make it feel deceptively cooler. Luckily, there's at least one covered bar (and often an ice cream stand) at virtually every hotel you pass. If you take the stroll at night, you can hotel-hop for dinner, dancing, gambling, and late-night entertainment. On the north side of the island, heavy trade winds make the waters too choppy for swimming, but the vistas are great and the terrain is wonderfully suited to sunbathing and geological explorations.

Baby Beach. On the island's eastern tip, this semicircular beach borders a bay that is as placid as a wading pool and only 4–5 ft deep—perfect for tots and terrible swimmers. Thatched shaded areas are good for cooling off. You may occasionally find topless sunbathers here.

Boca Grandi. Just west of Bachelor's Beach, on the northwest coast (near the Seagrape Grove and the Aruba Golf Club), Boca Grandi is excellent for wave jumping and windsurfing. Strong swimming skills are a must here.

Boca Prins. Near the Fontein Cave and Blue Lagoon, this beach is about as large as a Brazilian bikini, but with two rocky cliffs and tumultuously crashing waves, it's as romantic as you get in Aruba. This is not a swimming beach, however. Boca Prins is famous for its backdrop of enormous vanilla sand dunes, on which locals make a sport of dune sliding. You'll need a four-wheel drive to make the trek here. Bring a picnic lunch, a beach blanket, and sturdy sneakers.

Eagle Beach. Across the highway from what is quickly becoming known as Time-Share Lane is Eagle Beach, on the south coast. Not long ago it was a nearly deserted stretch of pristine sands dotted with the occasional thatched picnic hut. Now that the time-share resorts are completed, this beach is one of the more hopping ones on the island.

Fisherman's Hut. Next to the Holiday Inn, this beach is a windsurfer's haven. Take a picnic lunch (tables are available) and watch the elegant sails tame the wind.

Grapefield Beach. To the north of San Nicolas, this gorgeous beach is perfect for advanced windsurfing.

Malmok Beach. On the northwestern shore, this lackluster beach, also known as Boca Catalina, borders shallow waters that stretch out 300 yards from shore, making it perfect for beginners learning to windsurf. Right off the coast here is a favorite haunt for divers—the wreck of the German ship *Antilla,* scuttled in 1940.

Manchebo Beach (formerly Punta Brabo Beach). In front of the Manchebo Beach Resort, this impressively wide stretch of white powder attracts topless sunbathers. Going topless is not permitted in Aruba (though officials rarely enforce the ban here or at Baby Beach).

Palm Beach. Once called one of the 10 best beaches in the world by the *Miami Herald,* this is the stretch behind the Americana Aruba, Aruba Hilton Hotel and Casino, Aruba Palm Beach, and Holiday Inn hotels. It's the center of Aruban tourism, offering the best in swimming, sailing, and fishing. During high season, however, it's a sardine can.

Rodger's Beach. Next to Baby Beach on the eastern tip of the island, this is a beautiful curving stretch of sand only slightly marred by the view of the oil refinery at the far side of the bay.

OUTDOOR ACTIVITIES AND SPORTS

Bowling

Bowling is a very popular sport among locals. An international tournament is held in late spring, and a youth international tournament takes place in late summer. The **Eagle Bowling Palace** (⊠ Pos Abou, ☎ 297/8–35038) hosts both events and has 12 lanes, a cocktail lounge, and a snack bar; it's open 10 AM to 2 AM. Games run $5.75–$11.20, depending on the time of play.

Fishing

Many hotels can arrange a fishing-boat charter for you. The cost for a half-day outing usually runs $40 per person. You split your catch with the captain, who then sells his share to local restaurants. Bring your prize fish to a hotel restaurant where for a minimal fee (about US$6) it will become your meal.

With catches including barracuda, kingfish, bonito, wahoo, and black and yellow tuna, deep-sea fishing is great sport on Aruba. Annual championships are held in October at the **Aruba Nautical Club** (☎ 297/8–53022). Many charter boats are available for a half- or full-day sail. **De Palm Tours** (☎ 297/8–24400 or 800/766–6016, ⅢX 297/8–23012) can arrange trips for up to six people, in a variety of boat sizes and styles. Half-day tours, including all equipment, soft drinks, and boxed lunch, are about $250 for up to four people; full-day tours run about $500. **Pelican Tours** (☎ 297/8–31228 or 297/8–24739) and **Red Sail Sports** (☎ 297/8–61603) also arrange deep-sea-fishing charters.

Golfing

An 18-hole, par-71 golf course, **Tierra del Sol** (⊠ Malmokweg, ☎ 297/8–67800), opened in 1995 on the northwest coast near the California Lighthouse. Designed by Robert Trent Jones, Jr., the 6,811-yard championship course combines Aruba's native beauty—its flora, cacti, and rock formations—with the lush greens of the world's best courses. The Aruba Aces Championship, a Senior PGA tour event, takes place in January. The $120 greens fee includes a golf cart. Club rentals are $25–$45. Half-day "No Embarrassment" golf clinics, a bargain at $40, include lunch in the clubhouse. The Ventanas del Mar restaurant (☞ Chapter 3) in the clubhouse is worth a visit in its own right.

Aruba Golf Club (✉ Golfweg 82, near San Nicolas, ☎ 297/8–42006) has a nine-hole course with 20 sand traps and five water traps, roaming goats, and lots of cacti. There are 11 AstroTurf greens, making 18-hole tournaments a possibility. The clubhouse contains a bar and men's and women's locker rooms. The course's official U.S. Golf Association rating is 67; greens fees are $7.50 for 9 holes, $10 for 18 holes. Caddies and club rentals are available.

Two elevated 18-hole minigolf courses surrounded by a moat are available at **Joe Mendez Adventure Golf** (✉ Sasakiweg, ☎ 297/8–76625). There are also paddleboats and bumper boats, a bar, and a snack stand. A round of minigolf is $6.50 per 18 holes. It's open weekdays 5 PM–11 PM and weekends noon–11 PM.

Hiking

There are no marked trails through the **Arikok National Wildlife Park,** but that doesn't mean you can't blaze your own. Watch for snakes in this arid landscape, and carry water with you. Wild donkeys, goats, rabbits, parakeets, and a plethora of lizards (even the occasional iguana) will be your companions. The park is crowned by 577-ft Mt. Arikok, so climbing is also a possibility.

De Palm Tours (✉ L. G. Smith Blvd. 142, ☎ 297/8–24400 or 800/766–6016, FAX 297/8–23012) offers a guided three-hour trip to remote sites of unusual natural beauty accessible only on foot. The fee is $25 per person, including refreshments and transportation; a minimum of four people is required.

Horseback Riding

There are three ranches offering riding on the island, some taking you on jaunts along the beach, others on longer trail rides through countryside flanked by cacti, divi-divi trees, and aloe vera plants. **De Palm Tours** (⊠ L. G. Smith Blvd. 142, ☎ 297/8–24400 or 800/766–6016, 𝔽𝔸𝕏 297/8–23012) books them all with advance reservations; rates run about $20 for an hour-long countryside tour, $35 for a two-hour beach tour. Wear a hat and take lots of suntan lotion.

Land Sailing

Carts with a Windsurfer-type sail are rented at **Aruba Sail-Cart** (⊠ Bushiri 23, ☎ 297/8–35133) at $15 (single seater) and $20 (double seater) for 30 minutes of speeding across a dirt field. The sport is new to Aruba and thrilling for land-bound sailors. Anyone can learn the rudiments of driving the cart in just a few minutes. Rentals are available from 9 AM to sunset; food and drinks are served until 10 PM.

Parasailing

Motorboats from Eagle and Palm beaches tow people wearing parachute-like contraptions up and over the water for about 15 minutes ($40 for a single seater, $70 for a tandem).

Snorkeling and Scuba Diving

With visibility up to 90 ft, Aruban waters are excellent for snorkeling in shallow waters, and scuba divers will discover exotic marine life and coral, including manta rays, barracudas, and the rare green moray. With 42 major sites from which to choose, certified divers can go wall diving or reef diving—or explore wrecks sunk during World War II.

Prices are generally comparable among the better snorkeling and scuba-diving operators on the island. Expect snorkel gear to rent for about $15 per day, snorkeling trips to cost about $25. Scuba rates are not much more, at about $30 for a one-tank reef or wreck dive, $45 for a two-tank dive, $35 for a night dive.

Learning to dive with a reputable instructor is a must. In addition to training you how to resurface slowly enough to avoid "the bends"—a painful and potentially fatal condition caused by the accumulation of nitrogen bubbles in the bloodstream—a qualified instructor can teach you to read dive tables, the charts that calculate how long you can safely stay at certain depths. Resorts and dive shops offer three-hour introductory scuba diving courses for an average of $70 and week-long complete open-water certification for about $300. The short course involves both instruction on land and time in a pool or waist-deep water to get accustomed to the mouthpiece and hose (known as the regulator) and the mask. A shallow 20 ft dive from a boat or beach follows, supervised by the instructor.

The following major accredited diving organizations offer coursework towards earning a certification card—often called a C-card: NAUI (National Association of Underwater Instructors), CMAS (Confederation Mondiale des Activités Subaquatiques, which translates into World Underwater Federation), NASE (National Association of Scuba Educators), and PADI (Professional Association of Diving Instructors). PADI (⊠ 1251 E. Dyer Rd., #100, Santa Ana, CA 92705) offers a free list of training facilities.

While scuba (which stands for "self-contained underwater breathing apparatus") looks and is surprisingly simple, *call your physician before your vacation and make sure that you don't have some condition that should prevent you from diving!* A full checkup is an excellent idea, especially if you're over 30. Since it can be dangerous to travel on a plane within 24 hours of diving, you should schedule both your diving courses and travel plans accordingly.

Operators

Among the top scuba operators in Aruba are **Aruba Pro Dive** (⊠ Ponton 88, ☏ 297/8–25520), **Charlie's S.E.A. Scuba** (⊠ San Nicholas, ☏ 297/8–45086), **Scuba Aruba** (⊠ Seaport Mall, ☏ 297/8–34142), and **Mermaid Sports Divers** (⊠ Manchebo Beach Resort, ☏ 297/8–35546).

De Palm Tours (⊠ L. G. Smith Blvd. 142, ☏ 297/8–24400 or 800/766–6016, FAX 297/8–23012) offers daily snorkeling and scuba-diving trips. However, its rates ($30–$45) are the most expensive on the island.

Pelican Watersports (✉ Holiday Inn Beach Resort, ☎ 297/8–63600) offers snorkeling and scuba diving, as well as scuba instruction and certification. It also offers wreck and night dives at reasonable rates.

Red Sail Sports (✉ L. G. Smith Blvd. 83, ☎ 297/8–61603) offers scuba packages, resort courses, PADI-certification courses, night diving, and underwater camera rental.

Dive Sites

The *Antilla*—a brand new German freighter purposefully sunk by the Germans in 1945—is a favorite spot with divers and snorkelers. At 400 ft long, it is the largest wreck in the Caribbean, and its compartments are great for penetrations. It lies off the northwest coast near Malmok Beach.

Beginning divers can snap away (only with their cameras, that is) at the corals and parrot fish at **Arashi Reef**; at 35–40 ft, the reef is at an ideal depth for photography. It's near the northwest tip of the island, just above the *Antilla* wreck.

The *California* wreck is nearly 100 years old and is the infamous ship that received (but did not respond to) the *Titantic's* S.O.S signals. Is this nautical revenge? At a depth of 30–45 ft, the wreck and its large coral formations and tropical fish are perfect for underwater photography. However, it is for advanced divers only, due to choppy water and strong windward-side currents at Aruba's northeast tip.

Another great spot for novice divers is an oil tanker sunk by a German submarine in World War II: the *Pedernales.* The wreck's cabins, lavatories, and pipeline system are separated by coral formations. Two pieces of the ship were salvaged by the U.S. military to create a smaller vessel, which joined the fleet that invaded Normandy—another ironic example of vengeance. The wreck is near Palm Beach.

The **Tugboat** wreck is off Druif Beach and is one of the best of Aruba's dive sites. It drops gradually from 40 ft to 90 ft through gorgeous variations of coral and is home to two green morays.

Kantil Reef is a fun drop off site just south of Oranjestad, with huge boulders of brain and star coral, sea fans, and gorgoneas. You'll be in the company of much marine life here, including yellow tails, morays, and manta rays.

Porto Chiquito, at 20–80 ft, is known for its diversity of corals and sea life and is well worth visiting, especially since it's easy to access by car (it's near Savaneta). Manta rays and turtles can be spotted among the corals.

Tennis

Aruba's winds add a certain challenge to the best of swings, but world-class tennis has just arrived, at the **Aruba Racquet Club** (☎ 297/8–60215). The $1.4 million club was designed by Stan Smith Design International and is near the Aruba Marriott. There are eight tennis courts (six lighted), which are usually available, as well as a swimming pool, an aerobics center, and a restaurant on the grounds. Court fees are $10 per hour.

Windsurfing

Cool trade winds make Aruba the "windsurfing capital of the world." Aruba hosts the annual Hi-Winds Amateur World Challenge each year, an event that attracts hundreds of windsurfers from around the world.

Pelican Watersports (⊠ Holiday Inn Beach Resort, ☎ 297/8–63600) rents equipment and offers instruction with a certified Mistral instructor. Stock and custom boards rent for $40 per two hours, $60 per day. Pelican offers lessons three times a day; call for a schedule.

Red Sail Sports (⊠ L. G. Smith Blvd. 83, ☎ 297/8–61603) offers two-hour beginner lessons for $45 ($60 for two people). It also rents Fanatic boards and regular windsurfing boards by the hour, day, and week.

Windsurfing instruction and board rental are also available through **Sailboard Vacation** (⊠ L. G. Smith Blvd. 462, ☎ 297/8–61072), **Roger's Windsurf Place** (⊠ L. G. Smith Blvd. 472, ☎ 297/8–61918), and **De Palm Tours** (⊠ L. G.

Smith Blvd. 142, ☎ 297/8–24400 or 800/766–6016, FAX 297/8–23012). Complete vacation packages for windsurfers are also provided through all of the above operators.

5 Shopping

In case you want to be welcomed there.

We're here to see that you're always welcomed at establishments everywhere. That's why millions of people carry the American Express® Card – for peace of mind, confidence, and security, around the world or just around the corner.

do more ®

Cards

In case you're
running low.

We're here to help with more than 118,000 Express Cash
locations around the world. In order to enroll, just
call American Express before you start
your vacation.

do more

**Express
Cash**

And just in case.

We're here with American Express® Travelers Cheques and Cheques *for Two*.® They're the safest way to carry money on your vacation and the surest way to get a refund, practically anywhere, anytime.
Another way we help you...

do more®

AMERICAN EXPRESS

Travelers Cheques

ARUBA'S CHIEF SHOPPING STREET— Caya G. F. Betico Croes—makes for a pleasant diversion from the beach and casino life. *Duty-free* is a magic word here. Major credit cards are welcome virtually everywhere, U.S. dollars are accepted almost as often as local currency, and traveler's checks can be cashed with proof of identity. Shopping malls have arrived in Aruba, so when you finish walking the main street, stop in at a mall to browse through the chic boutiques.

Aruba's souvenir and crafts stores are full of Dutch porcelains and figurines, as befits the island's Netherlands heritage. Dutch cheese is a good buy (you are allowed to bring up to 1 pound of hard cheese through U.S. Customs), as are hand-embroidered linens and any products made from the native aloe vera plant—sunburn cream, face masks, and skin refreshers. There are also plenty of imports from all of the world, particulary from South America. Since there is no sales tax, the price you see on the tag is the price you pay. Don't try to bargain. Arubans consider it rude to haggle, despite what you may hear to the contrary.

Specialty Shops

HANDEMADE CRAFTS

At **Artesania Aruba** (⊠ L. G. Smith Blvd. 178, ☎ 297/8–37494) you'll find charming Aruban home-crafted pottery, silk-screened T-shirts and wall hangings, and folklore objects. There's a kiosk in the shopping district on Betico Croes as well.

The **Artistic Boutique** (⊠ Caya G. F. Betico Croes 25, ☎ 297/8–23142; ⊠ Aruba Hilton, ☎ 297/8–64466, ext. 3508; ⊠ Seaport Village Mall, ☎ 297/8–32567; ⊠ Holiday Inn, ☎ 297/8–33383) sells Aruban hand-embroidered linens, gold and silver jewelry, Persian carpets and dhurries, porcelain and pottery from Spain, and lots of antiques.

Art and Tradition Handicrafts (⊠ Caya G. F. Betico Croes 30, ☎ 297/8–36534) sells intriguing items that look hand-painted but aren't. Buds from the mopa mopa tree are boiled to form a resin, to which artists add vegetable colors. This resin is then stretched by hand and mouth. Tiny pieces are cut and layered to form intricate designs on wooden shapes—truly unusual gifts.

Creative Hands (⊠ Socotorolaan 5, Oranjestad, ☎ 297/8–35665) sells porcelain and ceramic *cunucu* houses and divi-divi trees, but the store's real draw is its exquisite Japanese dolls.

PERFUMES, COSMETICS AND CLOTHING

For duty-free perfumes and cosmetics, stop in at **Aruba Trading Company** (⊠ Caya G. F. Betico Croes 12, ☎ 297/8–22602), whose name is synonymous with old-fashioned reliability. ATC offers internationally known brand names at discounts, but you have to hunt for them. Perfumes and cosmetics are on the first floor, jewelry and men's and women's fashions are on the second.

Clothing is also sold at **Wulfsen & Wulfsen** (⊠ Caya G. F. Betico Croes 52, ☎ 297/8–23823). One of the highest-rated stores in the Netherlands Antilles for 25 years—and for much longer in Holland—Wulfsen's offers Italian, French, German, and Dutch fashions for both sexes. The Dutch line Mexx is a favorite of hip teens; Betty Barkley and Mondo are popular for women. Men's clothes range from the conservative to the wild.

J. L. Penha & Son's (⊠ Caya G. F. Betico Croes 11, ☎ 297/8–24161), another venerated name in Aruban merchandising, sells clothes, perfumes, and cosmetics and features Boucheron, Lanvin, Dior, and Cartier for women and Givenchy and Pierre Cardin for men.

Confetti (⊠ Seaport Mall, ☎ 297/8–37454) sells the hottest European and American swimsuits, cover-ups, beach hats, and other beach essentials.

JEWELRY AND WATCHES

For jewelry and watches, stop in at **Gandelman's Jewelers** (⊠ Caya G. F. Betico Croes 5-A, ☎ 297/8–34433) for Gucci and Swatch watches at reasonable prices, gold bracelets, pink and red coral, and a full line of Gucci accessories, from key chains to handbags. They have a customer service office in Connecticut (☎ 203/325–9786).

Little Switzerland (⊠ Caya G. F. Betico Croes 14, ☎ 297/8–21192; also locations in several hotel shopping arcades and in the new Royal Plaza Mall), the St. Thomas–based giant, has china, crystal, and fine tableware and offers good buys on Omega and Rado watches, Swarovski silver, Baccarat crystal, and Lladro figurines.

CIGARS

Cuban cigars are available at **La Casa Del Habano** (⊠ Royal Plaza Mall, ☎ 297/8–38503).

Shopping Malls

Newest on the bustling shopping scene is **Royal Plaza Mall** (⊠ L. G. Smith Blvd. 94), on the main drag just across from the cruise-ship terminal. Here you'll find cafés, a post office branch (open Monday–Saturday 7–5), and all the big-name chain stores, including Little Switzerland, Nautico, Tommy Hilfiger, and Gandelman's Jewelers. There's also the **Internet Café,** where you can sign on and send E-mail home and get your caffeine fix all in one stop.

Seaport Village Mall (⊠ L. G. Smith Blvd. across from the harbor, ☎ 297/8–36000) is landmarked by the Crystal Casino Tower. This covered mall is only five minutes from the cruise terminal. It has more than 120 stores, boutiques, and perfumeries, with merchandise to meet every taste and budget. The arcade is lined with tropical plants and caged parrots, and there is a casino at the top of the escalator. **Arti** has period-clad china dolls in a rainbow of skin tones. Made in Holland, the dolls stand 12–18 inches tall. Clown dolls in satin and lace and a very unusual tiny clay orchestra are collector's items. **Les Accessoires** sells purses made in Florence and exclusive leather designs, with prices ranging from $85 to $600. Their Venezuelan pareus come in handy as pool cover-ups. If green fire is your passion, **Colombian Emeralds** is just above the inside and outside bridges to the mall. **Tropical Wave** has some nice Indonesian sculpture, in the back behind the junk, as well as handwoven duffel bags and sweaters from Ecuador. The **Seaport Cinema**

(☎ 297/8–3600), in Seaport Market Place, features six theaters showing the latest U.S. movies.

There are several other shopping malls in Oranjestad, all worth visiting. The **Holland Aruba Mall** (✉ Havenstraat 6) houses a collection of smart shops and eateries. Nearby are the **Strada I** and **Strada II,** two small complexes of shops in tall Dutch buildings painted in pastels. Strada II is home to **Fendi,** whose Etrusco striped vinyl luggage is available at a 45% discount.

Port of Call Marketplace (✉ L. G. Smith Blvd. 17, ☎ 297/8–36706) features fine jewelry, perfumes, duty-free liquors, batiks, crystal, leather goods, and fashionable clothing.

For late-night shopping, head to the **Alahambra Casino Shopping Arcade** (✉ L. G. Smith Blvd. 47, ☎ 297/8–35000), open 5 PM–midnight. Souvenir shops, art boutiques, and fast-food outlets fill the arcade attached to the busy casino.

6 Nightlife

Casinos

CASINOS ARE ALL THE RAGE in Aruba. The crowds seem to flock to the newest of the new: Marriott's 10,700-square-ft **Stellaris Casino** (⊠ L. G. Smith Blvd. 101, ☎ 297/8–69000) is the latest dazzler on the high-roller scene. Prior to its opening, Sonesta's 24-hour **Crystal Casino** (⊠ L. G. Smith Blvd. 82, ☎ 297/8–36000) enjoyed the business until the Hyatt Regency expanded the ultramodern **Copacabana Casino** (⊠ J. E. Irausquin Blvd. 85, ☎ 297/8–61234), an enormous complex with a Carnival in Rio theme and live entertainment. Then it was the wildly popular **Royal Cabana Casino**—largest in the Caribbean—in La Cabana All Suite Beach Hotel (⊠ J. E. Irausquin Blvd. 250, ☎ 297/8–79000), with its sleek interior, multitheme three-in-one restaurant, and showcase Tropicana nightclub. Smart money's on the **Wyndham Casablanca Casino,** quietly elegant with a Bogart theme (⊠ J. E. Irausquin Blvd. 77, ☎ 297/8–64466). One place where you'll always find some action is the **Alhambra Casino** (⊠ L. G. Smith Blvd. 47, Oranjestad, ☎ 297/8–35000), where someone dressed as a Moorish slave gives every gambler a hearty handshake upon entering. The **Grand Holiday Casino** (⊠ Holiday Inn Beach Resort, J. E. Irausquin Blvd. 230, ☎ 297/8–67777) features sports betting in addition to the usual slots and table games. The **Royal Palm Casino** (⊠ J. E. Irausquin Blvd. 83, ☎ 297/8–64500) opens daily at 1 PM for slots, 5 PM for all other games. The **Aruba Palm Beach Hotel Casino** (⊠ J. E. Irausquin Blvd. 79, ☎ 297/8–63900) opens at 10 AM for slots, 6 PM for all other games. Low-key gambling can be found at the waterside **Seaport Casino** (⊠ L. G. Smith Blvd. 9, ☎ 297/8–35027).

For tips on gambling, *see* Chapter 9.

Discos and Dancing

Arubans usually start partying late, and action doesn't pick up till around midnight, mostly on the weekends. At the **Cellar** (⊠ Klipstraat 2, ☎ 297/8–26490) live bands perform Monday, Wednesday, Friday, and Saturday; you may hear blues, jazz, funk, reggae, or rock. For fresh air, head to the **Penthouse** bar area and dance floor on the roof. Another popular nightclub is **Cheers Café Bistro** (⊠ L. G. Smith Blvd. 17, ☎ 297/8–30838), in the Port of Call Marketplace near the pier. The dance floor is usually so packed that you can barely wiggle, and the party typically spills out onto the side porch.

New on the dancing scene is the round **Cobalt Club** (Royal Plaza Mall, L. G. Smith Blvd. 172, Oranjestad, ☎ 297/8–38381), atop the Royal Plaza Mall downtown, where merengue, salsa, *soca*, and other Latin and Caribbean tunes and indoor and outdoor bars keep the party moving. Also new is **City One** (⊠ Italiastraat 42, ☎ 297/8–33888), the island's largest disco, with a cavernous dance floor, two bars, and big-screen TVs that flash music videos and recently released films.

Specialty Theme Nights

Unique to Aruba's nightlife is the number of specialty theme nights offered by its hotels: At last count there were more than 30. Each "party" features a buffet dinner and entertainment, followed by dancing. Best bets are **Aruban Folkloric** on Friday at the Manchebo Beach Hotel, **Pirates Night** on Sunday at the Bucuti Beach Resort, **Brazilian Jungle Night** on Saturday at the Bushiri Beach Resort, and **Caribbean Carnival Royale** on Monday at the Costa Linda. The top show groups tend to rotate among the resorts, so there's bound to be something going on every night of the week. For a complete list, contact the Aruba Tourism Authority (☎ 297/8–60242).

An Aruban must is the **Bon Bini Festival,** held every Tuesday evening from 6:30 to 8:30 in the outdoor courtyard of the Fort Zoutman Museum. *Bon bini* is Papiamento for "welcome," and this tourist event is the Aruba Institute of Culture and Education's way of introducing you to all things Aruban. Stroll by the stands of Aruban foods, drinks, and crafts or watch Aruban entertainers perform Antillean music and folkloric dancing. A master of ceremonies explains the history of the dances, instruments, and music. It's a fun event and a good way to meet other tourists. Look for the clock tower. ⊠ *Oranjestraat,* ☎ *297/8–22185.* 🎫 *$3.*

Theater

Tropicana (⊠ J. E. Irausquin Blvd. 250, ☎ 297/8–69806), La Cabana All Suite's cabaret theater and nightclub, features first-class Las Vegas–style reviews and a special comedy series every weekend.

The **Wyndham Aruba** (⊠ J. E. Irausquin Blvd. 77, ☎ 297/8–64466) showcases an entertaining Cuban review from 8 to 10 PM Tuesday through Saturday in its theater. Arrive at 8 for dinner ($29 per person) or at 9 for cocktails only ($20 per person).

Twinklebone's House of Roast Beef (⊠ Noord 124, ☎ 297/8–26780) does serve succulent prime rib and the like. But it's best known for the fun impromptu cabaret of Carnival music put on by the staff every night but Sunday. Some customers find it hokey; others eat it up.

7 Exploring Aruba

ORANJESTAD, THE CAPITAL OF ARUBA, is good for shopping by day and dining by night, but the real Aruba—what's left of a wild, untamed beauty—can be found only in the countryside. Rent a car, take a sightseeing tour, or hire a cab for $25 an hour (for up to four people). The main highways are well paved, but on the windward side of the island some roads are still a mixture of compacted dirt and stones. Although a car is fine, a four-wheel drive will allow you to explore the unpaved interior. Traffic is sparse, and you can't get lost. If you do lose your way, just follow the divi-divi trees (because of the direction of the ever-present trade winds, the trees are bent toward the leeward side of the island, where all the hotels are). Signs leading to sights of interest are often small and hand-lettered, so watch closely (though this is slowly changing as the government puts up official road signs).

Few beaches outside the hotel strip have refreshment stands, so take your own food and drink. And one more caution: There are *no* public bathrooms—anywhere—once you leave Oranjestad, except in the infrequent restaurant.

Numbers in the margin correspond to points of interest on the Exploring Aruba map.

Sights to See

❽ Alto Vista Chapel. Alone near the northwest corner of the island sits the scenic little Alto Vista Chapel. The wind whistles through the simple mustard-color walls, eerie boulders, and looming cacti. Along the side of the road as you head back to civilization are miniature crosses painted with depictions of the Stations of the Cross and hand-lettered signs exhorting PRAY FOR US, SINNERS, and the like—a primitive yet powerful evocation of faith. To get there, follow the rough, winding dirt road that loops around the northern tip of the island, or from the hotel strip take Palm Beach Road through three intersections and watch for the asphalt road to the left just past the Alto Vista Rum Shop.

⑨ California Lighthouse. At the far north end of the island stands this closed lighthouse. It is surrounded by huge boulders that look like extraterrestrial monsters; in this stark landscape you'll feel as though you've just landed on the moon. There is a placard explaining the history of the lighthouse and the story of the wreck of the German ship *California* (just off the tip of the island here) next to the trattoria.

⑤ Caves. Anyone looking for geological exotica should head for the north coast, driving northwest from San Nicolas. Stop at the two old Indian caves **Guadirikiri** and **Fontein.** Both were used by the native Indians centuries ago (notice the fire mark in the ceiling); sadly, the cave walls are marred by modern graffiti. You may enter the caves, but there are no guides available, and bats are known to make appearances (not to worry—they won't bother you). Wear sneakers and take a flashlight or rent one from the soda vendor who has set up shop here. Just before the Fontein and Guadirikiri caves lies the **Tunnel of Love** (also known as Huiliba), a heart-shape tunnel containing naturally sculpted rocks whose individual appearances look just like the Madonna, Abe Lincoln, even a jaguar. The climb through the tunnel is strenuous and should not be attempted by anyone not in good physical condition; it's definitely not recommended for senior citizens or young children. Remember, admission is free to all three caves—don't be deterred by the occasionally pushy vendors.

③ Frenchman's Pass. A bit of history can be found along this dark, luscious stretch of road arbored by overhanging trees and bordered by towering cacti. Local legend claims that the French and native Indians warred here during the 17th century for control of the island. To get here, drive east on L. G. Smith Boulevard past a shimmering vista of blue-green sea toward San Nicolas, on what is known as the sunrise side of the island. Turn left where you see the drive-in theater (a popular hangout for Arubans), drive to the first intersection, turn right, and follow the curve to the right. Gold was discovered on Aruba in 1824, and nearby you'll find the massive cement-and-limestone ruins of the **Balashi Gold Smelter Ruins** (take the dirt road veering to the right)—a lovely place to picnic, listen to the parakeets, and contem-

52

Exploring Aruba

California Pt.

9 **California Sand Dunes**

10

Malmok Beach

Mt. Alto Vista

8

Fisherman's Hut
Palm Beach

Bushiribana○

○Noord

○Paradera

Eagle Beach

2

Manchebo Beach
Divi Beach
Druif Bay

Santa Cr

1

Oranjestad

Queen Beatrix International Airport

N

0   4 miles
0   6 km

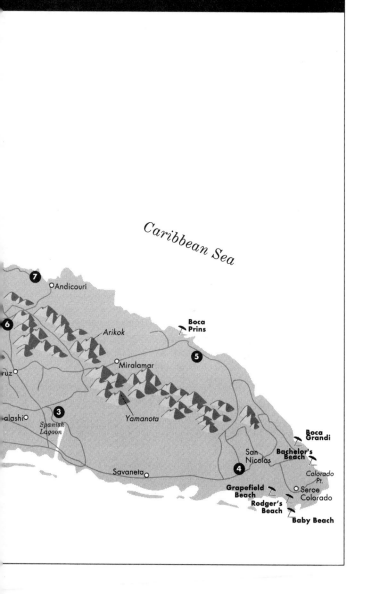

Caribbean Sea

○Andicouri

Arikok

**Boca
Prins**

○Miralamar

Yamanota

○ruz

○alashi

*Spanish
Lagoon*

Savaneta○

**Boca
Grandi**

San
Nicolas

**Bachelor's
Beach**

*Colorado
Pt.*

○ Seroe
Colorado

**Grapefield
Beach**

**Rodger's
Beach**

Baby Beach

plate the towering cacti. A magnificent gnarled divi-divi tree guards the entrance.

2 Hooiberg. This 541-ft peak, whose name translates as Haystack Hill, is inland just past the airport. If you have the energy, climb the 562 steps to the top for an impressive view of the city. On a clear day you can even see Venezuela. To get there from Oranjestad, turn onto Caya C. F. Croes (shown on island maps as 7A) toward Santa Cruz; the peak will be on your right.

10 Malmok. On the drive to the northern tip of the island you'll pass through Malmok, where Aruba's wealthiest families reside. Jutting above the water not far off Malmok Beach— one of the finest spots for shelling, snorkeling, and windsurfing, are parts of the wreck of the German ship *Antilla,* scuttled here in 1940.

7 Natural Bridge. This bridge, at the midway mark on the windward coast, was sculpted out of coral rock by centuries of raging wind and sea. To get to it, follow the main road inland (Hospitalstraat) and then the signs that lead the way. Just before you reach the Natural Bridge, you'll pass the massive and intriguing 19th-century stone ruins of the **Bushiribana Gold Smelter,** which resembles a crumbling fortress, and a section of surf-pounded coastline called Boca Mahose. Near the natural bridge is a café overlooking the water and a souvenir shop stuffed with trinkets, T-shirts, and postcards for reasonable prices.

1 Oranjestad. Aruba's charming Dutch capital is best explored on foot. There are many shopping malls with boutiques and shops. The palm-lined thoroughfare in the center of town runs between pastel-painted buildings, old and new, of typical Dutch design.

At the **Archaeology Museum** you'll find two rooms chockablock with fascinating Indian artifacts, farm and domestic utensils, and skeletons. Across the street you'll see a handsome Protestant church. ⊠ *Zoutmanstraat 1,* ☎ *297/8–28979.* ▣ *Free.* ☉ *Weekdays 8–noon and 1–4.*

One of the island's oldest buildings, **Fort Zoutman** was built in 1796 and used as a major fortress in the skirmishes between British and Curaçao troops. The Willem III Tower, named for the Dutch monarch of that time, was added in 1868. The fort's Historical Museum displays centuries' worth of Aruban relics and Caiquetio artifacts in an 18th-century Aruban house. ⊠ *Zoutmanstraat z/n,* ☏ *297/8–26099.* ▨ *$1.15.* ☉ *Weekdays 9–noon and 1:30–4:30.*

The tiny **Numismatic Museum,** next to St. Francis Roman Catholic Church, displays coins and paper money from more than 100 countries. ⊠ *Zuidstraat 7,* ☏ *297/8–28831.* ▨ *Free.* ☉ *Weekdays 7:30–noon and 1–4:30.*

❻ Rock Formations. The massive boulders at **Ayo** and **Casibari** are said to be a mystery since they don't match the geological makeup of the island. Whether they're a mystery or not, you can climb to the top for fine views of Aruba's arid countryside or to get snapshots of brown or blue lizards as you hike among the towering cacti that surround the formations. Climbing is not recommended for children or older visitors—there are no handrails on the way up, and you must climb through tunnels and on narrow steps and ledges to reach the top. At Ayo you'll find ancient pictographs in a small cave (the entrance is protected by iron bars to prevent vandalism of the artifacts). Access to Casibari is via Tanki Highway 4A and to Ayo is via Highway 6A; watch carefully for the turnoff signs near the center of the island on the way to the windward side.

❹ San Nicolas. During the heyday of the Exxon refineries, Aruba's oldest village was a bustling port; now it's dedicated to tourism, with the main-street promenade full of interesting kiosks. The **China Clipper Bar,** on Main Street, used to be a famous red-light bar frequented by sailors docked in port. Another institution is **Charlie's Bar** (☞ Chapter 3), a San Nicolas hangout for more than 50 years. Stop in for a drink and advice on what to do on this section of the island. The entire San Nicholas district is undergoing a massive revitalization project that will introduce parks, a cultural center, a central market, and an arts promenade, but it's hard to say what will be completed by 1998.

Guided Tours

Boat Cruises

If you try a cruise around the island, know that on choppy waters stirred up by the trade winds, trimarans give a much smoother ride than monohull boats. Sucking on lemon or lime candy may help a queasy stomach; avoid going with an empty stomach. The most popular and reputable sailing cruises are offered by **De Palm Tours** (☎ 297/8–24400 or 800/766–6016, FAX 297/8–23012), **Mi Dushi** (☎ 297/8–28919), **Red Sail Sports** (☎ 297/8–24500), **Pelican Watersports** (☎ 297/8–31228), **Pirate Cruises** (☎ 297/8–24554), and **Wave Dancer** (☎ 297/8–25520).

Moonlight cruises offer stunning views and cost about $25 per person. (Be prepared to sail with a lot of sappy honeymooners.) There is also a variety of snorkeling, dinner and dancing, and sunset party cruises to choose from, priced from $25 to $60 per person. Contact **Red Sail Sports** (☎ 297/8–24500), **Pelican Watersports** (☎ 297/8–31228), or **De Palm Tours** (☎ 297/8–24400 or 800/766–6016, FAX 297/8–23012). One favorite is the four-hour snorkel and sail cruise, with open bar and luch, aboard the *Mi Dushi,* a beautifully restored 1925 Swedish sailboat. This two-masted wooden vessel is captained by Mario Maduro and a fun crew who act as lifeguards, snorkel instructors, bartenders, galley staff, deckhands, and storytellers. Two stops are made for snorkeling; save your energy for the second one, at the wreck of the *Antilla* (☞ Snorkeling and Scuba Diving *in* Chapter 4). The cost is $45.

Orientation Tours

Aruba's highlights can be seen in a day. Although most highways are in excellent condition, signs and directions are haphazard, making a guided tour your best option for exploring if you have only a short time. **De Palm Tours** (✉ L. G. Smith Blvd. 142, ☎ 297/8–24400 or 800/766–6016, FAX 297/8–23012) has a near monopoly on the Aruban sightseeing business; reservations may be made through its general office or at hotel tour-desk branches. The basic 3½-hour tour hits the high spots of the island, including Santa Anna Church, the Casibari rock formation, the Natural Bridge, and the Gold Smelter ruins. Wear tennis or hiking shoes (there'll be optional climbing) and note that the air-conditioned bus can get cold. The tour, which begins at 9:30 AM, picks you up in your lobby and costs $20 per person. There's also a fun full-day Jeep Adventure tour ($55 per person) that hits some popular spots difficult to find on your own. Highlights include the California Lighthouse, Alto Vista Chapel, Guadiriki Cave in Arikok National Park, and lunch and snorkeling at De Palm's private island. Take a bandanna to cover your mouth, as the ride on rocky dirt roads can get quite dusty. De Palm also offers full-day tours of Caracas, Venezuela ($240, passport required), and Curaçao ($209; ☞ Guided Tours *in* Chapter 8). Prices include round-trip airfare, transfers, sightseeing, and lunch; there is also free time for shopping.

Aruba Friendly Tours (⊠ Cumana 20, Oranjestad, ☎ 297/8–23230, FAX 297/8–33074) also offers tours of Aruba's main sights.

Special-Interest Tours

For a tour of prehistoric Indian cultures, volcanic formations, and natural wildlife, contact archaeologist Egbert Boerstra of **Marlin Booster Tracking, Inc.,** at Charlie's Bar (☎ 297/8–41513). The fee for a four-hour tour is $50 per person, including a cold picnic lunch and beverages. Tours can be given in English, Dutch, German, Spanish, and French.

Hikers will enjoy a guided three-hour trip to remote sites of unusual natural beauty accessible only on foot. The fee is $25 per person, including refreshments and transportation; a minimum of four people is required. Contact **De Palm Tours** (☎ 297/8–24400 or 800/766–6016, FAX 297/8–23012).

You can now explore an underwater reef teeming with marine life without getting wet. **Atlantis Submarines** (⊠ Seaport Village Marina, ☎ 297/8–36090 or 800/253–0493) operates a 65-ft air-conditioned sub that takes 46 passengers 95–150 ft below the surface along Aruba's Barcadera Reef. The two-hour trip (including boat transfer to the submarine platform and 50-minute plunge) costs $70 for adults, $29 for children 4–16. If you are not a scuba diver, the hour in the submarine is the next best thing to being down among the fish and coral. Another option is the **Sea-**

world Explorer (☎ 297/8–62807), a semisubmersible that allows passengers to sit and view Aruba's marine habitat from 5 ft below the surface. Cost is $33 for the 1½-hour tour.

Colibri Helicopters (☎ 297/8–931832) offers a 20-minute Island Adventure tour that treats guests to a bird's-eye view of California Lighthouse, the sand dunes, the Gold Smelter ruins, the Natural Bridge, Oranjestad, and visiting cruise ships. Cost is $98 per person. A shorter 10-minute flight zooms over the beaches of the island and a sunken WWII freighter for $49 per person.

Romantic **horse-drawn carriage rides** through the city streets of Oranjestad run $30 for a 30-minute tour; hours of operation are 7 PM–11 PM, and rides depart from the clock tower at the Royal Plaza Mall.

8 Side Trip to Curaçao

CURAÇAO IS AN ISLAND FOR EXPLORERS. Its charming Dutch capital, underwater park, Seaquarium, floating market, and dozens of little cove beaches give it a taste of everything, and it is apt to please most tastes. Forty-two miles east of Aruba and 35 mi north of Venezuela, Curaçao, at 38 mi long and 2–7½ mi wide, is the largest island in the Netherlands Antilles. The sun smiles down on the island, but it's never stiflingly hot; as on Aruba, the gentle trade winds are always refreshing. Water sports attract enthusiasts from all over the world, and some of the best reef diving is here. Though the island claims 38 beaches, it doesn't have long stretches of silky sand; rather, beaches are rocky stretches of washed-up coral that eventually breaks down into smooth white or pink sand. The island is dominated by an arid countryside, rocky coves, and a sprawling capital built around a natural harbor. Tourism has become a major economic force in the past decade, with millions of dollars invested in restoring old colonial landmarks and modernizing hotels, but Curaçao's atmosphere remains comparatively low-key—offering an appealing alternative to the commercialism of many other islands.

As seen from the Otrabanda of Willemstad by the first-time visitor, Curaçao's "face" will be a surprise—spiffy rows of pastel-colored town houses that look transplanted from Holland. Although the gabled roofs and red tiles show a Dutch influence, the gay colors of the facades are peculiar to Curaçao. It is said that a popular governor suffered from migraines, a condition irritated by the color white, so all the houses were painted in colors. The dollhouse look of the landhouses or *landhuizen* (plantation houses) makes a cheerful contrast to the stark cacti and the austere shrubbery that dot the countryside.

The history books still cannot agree on who discovered Curaçao, but they agree that it was around 1499. The first Spanish settlers arrived in 1527. The Dutch came in 1634 via the Netherlands West India Company and promptly shipped off the Spaniards and the few remaining Indians—survivors of the battles for ownership of the island, famine, and disease—to Venezuela. Eight years later, Peter Stuyvesant began his rule as governor, which lasted until he left for New York around 1645. Twelve Jewish families arrived from Amsterdam in 1651, and by 1732 there was a synagogue; the present structure is the oldest synagogue still in use in the Western Hemisphere. Over the years, the city built massive fortresses to defend against French and British invasions—many of those ramparts now house unusual restaurants and hotels. The Dutch claim to Curaçao was finally recognized in 1815 by the Treaty of Paris. In 1954 Curaçao became an autonomous part of the Kingdom of the Netherlands, with a governor appointed by the queen, an elected parliament, and an island council.

Today Curaçao's population is derived from more than 50 nationalities in an exuberant mix of Latin, European, and African roots and a Babel of tongues, resulting in superb restaurants and an active cultural scene.

Exploring Curaçao

Willemstad, the capital in the southern half of the island, is cut in two by Santa Anna Bay. There are three ways to make the crossing from one side to the other: (1) drive or take a taxi over the Juliana Bridge, (2) traverse the Queen Emma Pontoon Bridge on foot, or (3) ride the free ferry, which runs when the Pontoon bridge is open for passing ships.

The Weg Maar Santa Cruz road through the village of Soto winds to the northwest tip of the island through landscape that Georgia O'Keeffe might have painted—towering cacti, flamboyant dried shrubbery, and aluminum-roof houses. Throughout this *cunucu,* or countryside, you'll see native fishermen hauling in their nets, women pounding cornmeal, and an occasional donkey blocking traffic. Landhouses, large plantation houses from centuries past, dot the countryside, though most are closed to the public. Their facades, however, can often be glimpsed from the highway. To explore the eastern side of the island, take the coastal road—Martin Luther King Boulevard—from Willemstad about 2 mi to Bapor Kibra. Here you'll find the Seaquarium and the Underwater Park.

62

Curaçao Exploring and Dining

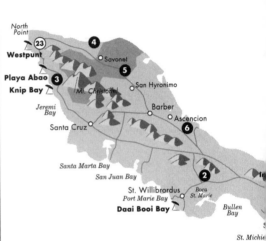

North Point

Westpunt

Playa Abao

Knip Bay

Savonet

San Hyronimo

Mt. Christoffel

Jeremi Bay

Santa Cruz

Barber

Ascencion

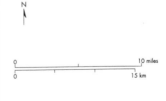

Santa Marta Bay

San Juan Bay

St. Willibrordus
Port Marie Bay

Daai Booi Bay

Boca St. Marie

Bullen Bay

St. Michie

Blauw

N

0   10 miles

0   15 km

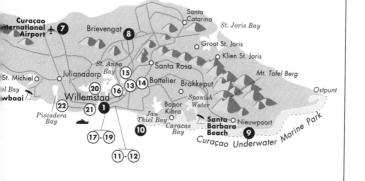

Caribbean Sea

Curaçao International Airport ✈ **7**

Brievengat **8**

Santa Catarina

St. Joris Bay

Groot St. Joris

Klien St. Joris

St. Anna Bay

15

Santa Rosa

Bottelier

Brakkeput

Mt. Tafel Berg

St. Michiel ○

Juliandorp ○

20

13 **14**

16

Ostpunt

l Bay
wbaai

22

Willemstad

21 **1**

Bapor Kibra

Spanish Water

Nieuwpoort

Piscadera Bay

10

Jan Thiel Bay

Caracas Bay

Santa ○
Barbara Beach

9

17-**19**

11-**12**

Curaçao Underwater Marine Park

Numbers in the margin correspond to points of interest on the Curaçao map.

SIGHTS TO SEE

④ Boca Tabla. At Boca Tabla, the sea has carved a magnificent grotto. Safely tucked in the back, you can watch and listen to the waves crashing ferociously against the rocks. ⌂ *Westpunt Hwy., just past village of Soto.*

★ **⑤ Christoffel Park.** This fantastic 4,450-acre garden and wildlife preserve centers on the towering Mt. Christoffel. The park consists of three former plantations with individual trails that take about 1 to 1½ hours each to traverse. You may drive your own car (if it has heavy-treaded wheels) or rent a four-wheel drive with an accompanying guide (NAf150 for up to five passengers). Start out early (by 10 AM the park starts to feel like a sauna), and if you're going solo, first study the *Excursion Guide to Christoffel Park* sold at the front desk of the elegant, if dilapidated, Landhuis Savonet (the plantation house turned Natural History Museum); it outlines the various routes and identifies the flora and fauna found here. There is a 20-mi network of roads that will treat you to views of hilly fields full of prickly-pear cacti, divi-divi trees, bushy-haired palms, and exotic flowers that bloom after November showers. There are also caves—the brave will revel in the rustling of bat wings and the sight of scuttling scorpion spiders (not poisonous)—and ancient Indian drawings.

As you drive, keep a lookout for tiny deer, goats, and small wildlife that might suddenly dart in front of your car. The whip snakes and minute silver snakes you may encounter are not poisonous. White-tail hawks may be seen on the green route, white orchids and crownlike passionflowers on the yellow route. Climbing the 1,239-ft Mt. Christoffel on foot is an exhilarating experience and a definite challenge to anyone who hasn't grown up scaling the Alps. The park's guidebook claims the round-trip will take you one hour, and Curaçaoan adolescent boys do make a sport of racing up and down, but it's really more like two (sweaty) hours from the base of the mountain for a reasonably fit person who's not an expert hiker. The view from the peak, however, *is* thrilling—a panorama of the island, including Santa Marta Bay and the tabletop mountain of St. Hironimus. On a clear day, you can even see the mountain ranges of Venezuela, Bonaire, and Aruba. ⊠ *Savonet,* ☎ *5999/864–0363.* ☞ *Park and museum $9, museum only $3.* ☉ *Mon.–Sat. 8–4, Sun. 6–3; last admittance 1 hr before closing.*

❻ Country House Museum. This thatched-roof cottage is a living museum demonstrating 19th-century country life. It's filled with antique furniture, farm implements, and clothing typical of colonial life on the island. Out back is a minifarm with penned donkeys, caged parrots, eagles, and iguana. Look closely at the fence—it's made of living cacti. There's also a snack bar. A festival featuring live music and local crafts takes place here on the first Sunday of each month. ⊠ *Dokterstuin 27,* ☎ *5999/864–2742.* ☞ *$1.50.* ☉ *Tues.–Fri. 9–4, weekends 9–5.*

❿ Curaçao Seaquarium. The Seaquarium is *the* place to see the island's underwater treasures without getting your feet wet. It's the world's only public aquarium where sea creatures are raised and cultivated totally by natural methods. Where else can you hand-feed a shark (or watch a diver do it)? The **Animal Encounters** section consists of a broad, 12-ft-deep open-water enclosure that brings you face to face with a variety of jaws. Snorkelers and divers are welcome to swim freely with stingrays, tarpon, groupers, and such. Diving instruction and equipment are part of the package; it's a thrilling introduction to the sport in a controlled environment. The highlight for most is the variety of sharks in one section of the enclosure, safely divided off by mesh fencing and thick Plexiglas; divers and snorkelers can feed the sharks by hand in perfect safety through holes in the Plexiglas and the faint-hearted can watch from an underwater observatory. The cost is $55 for divers, $30 for snorkelers, which includes admission to the Seaquarium, training in snorkeling and scuba diving, use of equipment, and food for the fish, turtles, and sharks. Reservations for Animal Encounters must be made 24 hours in advance.

You can spend several hours mesmerized by the 46 freshwater tanks full of more than 400 varieties of exotic fish and vegetation found in the waters around Curaçao, including sharks, lobsters, turtles, corals, and sponges. Look out for the more than 5-ft-long mascot, Herbie the lugubrious jewfish. One outdoor enclosure houses a sea lion and a sea bear (yes, they're different, like a horse and a mule). There are also glass-bottom-boat tours, fun feeding shows, and a viewing platform overlooking the wreck of the steamship SS *Oranje Nassau*, which sank in 1906 and now sits in 10 ft of water. A nearby 495-yard man-made beach is well suited to novice swimmers and children, and bathroom and shower facilities are available. A souvenir shop sells some of the best postcards and coral jewelry on the island. ⊠ *Bapor Kibra*, ☎ *5999/461–6666*, FAX *5999/461– 3671.* 🖾 *$13.25.* ☉ *Daily 8:30–6.*

⑨ Curaçao Underwater Marine Park. About 12½ mi of untouched coral reefs have been granted the status of national park. Mooring buoys placed at the most interesting dive sites on the reef provide safe anchoring and prevent damage to the reef. Several sunken ships lie awaiting visitors in the deep. The park stretches along the south shore from the Princess Beach Hotel in Willemstad to the eastern tip of the island. ⊠ *Off southeast shore.*

⑦ Hato Caves. Hour-long guided tours wind down into various chambers to the water pools, voodoo chamber, wishing well, fruit bats' sleeping quarters, and Curaçao Falls, where a stream of silver joins with a stream of gold (they're colored by lights) and is guarded by a limestone "dragon" perched nearby. Hidden lights illuminate the limestone formations and gravel walkways. This is one of the better Caribbean caves open to the public, but keep in mind that there are 49 steep steps to reach the entrance, and the cave itself is dank and hot (though they've put electric fans in some areas to provide relief). ⊠ *Head northwest toward airport, take right onto Gosieweg, follow loop right onto Schottegatweg, take another right onto Jan Norduynweg, a final right onto Rooseveltweg, and follow signs,* ☎ *5999/ 868–0379.* 🖾 *$6.25.* ☉ *Daily 10–5.*

⑧ Landhuis Brievengat. This mustard-colored plantation house is a fine example of the island's past. You can see the original kitchen still intact, the 18-inch-thick walls, fine antiques, and the watch towers once used for lovers' trysts. The restaurant, open only on Wednesday and Friday, serves a fine rijstaffel. Friday night a party is held on the wide wraparound terrace, with two bands and plenty to drink ($6 cover charge). ⊠ *10-min drive northeast of Willemstad,*

near Centro Deportivo sports stadium, ☎ *5999/737–8344.*
🖾 *$1.* ☺ *Mon.–Sat. 9:15–12:15 and 3–6.*

② **Landhuis Jan Kok.** For a splendid view, and some unusual
island tales of ghosts, visit this mid-17th-century plantation house overlooking the salt pans. Since the hours are
irregular, be sure to call ahead to arrange a tour of this re-
putedly haunted house, or stop by on Sunday mornings,
when the proprietor occasionally opens the small restaurant behind her home and serves delicious Dutch pancakes.
🖾 *Weg Naar San Willibrordus,* ☎ *5999/864–8087.* 🖾 *$3.*
☺ *Weekdays 11 AM–8 PM, but call ahead to arrange tour.*

③ **Landhuis Knip.** In terms of the number of slaves held, this
was the largest plantation on the island in its prime. It therefore comes as no surprise that the slave revolt took place
here in 1795. The renovated plantation house near the
western tip of the island is filled with period furnishings,
clothing, and other household goods. You can also walk
around the extensive stables and barns used in the opera-
tion of this maize plantation. 🖾 *Weg Naar Santa Cruz,* ☎
5999/864–0244. 🖾 *$2; free Sun.* ☺ *Sun.–Fri. 9–noon
and 2–4.*

Willemstad

① What does **Willemstad,** the capital of Curaçao, have in com-
mon with New York City? Broadway, for one. Here it's called
Breedestraat, but the origin is the same. Dutch settlers came
here in the 1630s, the same period when they sailed through
the Narrows to Manhattan, bringing with them original red-
tile roofs, first used on the trade ships as ballast and later
incorporated into the architecture of Willemstad.

Willemstad is a favorite cruise stop for two reasons: The
shopping is considered among the best in the Caribbean,
and a quick tour of most of the downtown sights can be
managed within a six-block radius. Santa Anna Bay slices
the city down the middle: On one side is the Punda, and
on the other is the Otrabanda (literally, the "other side").
Think of the Punda as the side for tourists, crammed with
shops, restaurants, monuments, and markets. Otrabanda
is less touristy, with lots of narrow, winding streets full of
private homes notable for their picturesque gables and
Dutch-influenced designs.

SIGHTS TO SEE

Curaçao Museum. Housed in a century-old former plantation house, this small museum is filled with artifacts, paintings, and antique furnishings that trace the island's history. This is also the venue for art exhibitions that visit the island. ⊠ *Leeuwenhoekstraat,* ☎ *5999/462–3873.* 🎫 *$2.25.* ⊙ *Weekdays 9–noon and 2–5, Sun. 10–4.*

Floating Market. Each morning dozens of Venezuelan schooners laden with tropical fruits and vegetables arrive at this bustling market on the Punda side of the city. Fresh mangoes, papayas, and exotic vegetables vie for space with freshly caught fish and herbs and spices. The buying is best at 6:30 AM, but there's plenty of action to see throughout the afternoon. Any produce bought here, however, should be thoroughly washed before eating. Note: At press time the floating market was temporarily located across Waaigat Channel while the city renovated the dock area. ⊠ *Sha Caprileskade.*

Fort Amsterdam. Step through the archway and enter another century. The entire structure dates from the 1700s, when it was the center of the city and the most important fort on the island. Now it houses the governor's residence, the Fort Church, the ministry, and other government offices. Outside the entrance a series of majestic gnarled *wayaka* trees are fancifully carved with a dragon, a giant squid, and a mermaid—the work of noted local artist Mac Alberto, who can be seen strolling the streets impeccably garbed in blinding white suits, a courtly boutonniere in his lapel. ⊠ *Foot of Queen Emma Bridge.*

Mikveh Israel-Emanuel Synagogue. This synagogue was dedicated in 1732 by the Jewish community that originally came from Amsterdam in 1651 to establish a new congregation. Jews from Portugal and Brazil, fleeing persecution, soon joined them, and by the early 1700s more than 2,000 Jews were in residence. This temple, the oldest still in use in the Western Hemisphere, is one of the most important sights in Curaçao and draws 20,000 visitors a year. Enter through the Spanish-tiled courtyard around the corner from Columbusstraat on Hanchi Di Snoa, and ask the front office to direct you to the guide on duty. A unique feature is the brilliant white sand covering the synagogue floor, a remembrance of Moses leading his people through the desert and of the Diaspora. The Hebrew letters on the four pillars signify the names of the Four Mothers of Israel: Sarah, Rebecca, Rachel, and Leah. The fascinating **Jewish Cultural Museum** (☎ 5999/461–1633) in the back displays Jewish antiques and artifacts from Jewish families collected from all over the world. The gift shop has excellent postcards and commemorative medallions. English and Hebrew services are held Friday at 6:30 PM and Saturday at 10 AM. Men who attend should wear a jacket and tie. ⊠ *Hanchi Di Snoa 29,* ☎ *5999/461–1067.* ⌨ *Small donation expected in synagogue; Jewish Cultural Museum $2.* ☉ *Weekdays 9–11:45 and 2:30–5 (closing time depends on schedule of services).*

Old Market (Marche). Behind the post office is where you'll find local women preparing hearty Antillean lunches at the Old Market. For $4–$6 you can enjoy such Curaçaoan specialties as *funchi* (corn bread), *keshi yena* (Gouda cheese stuffed with meat), goat stew, fried fish, peas and rice, and fried plantains. ⊠ *De Ruyterkade.*

Plaza Piar. This plaza, next to Fort Amsterdam, was dedicated to Manuel Piar, a native Curaçaoan who fought for the independence of Venezuela under the liberator Simon Bolívar. On one side of the plaza is the **Waterfort,** a bastion dating from 1634. The original cannons are still positioned in the battlements. The foundation, however, now forms the walls of the Van Der Valk Plaza Hotel.

Queen Emma Bridge. This bridge is affectionately called the Swinging Old Lady by the natives. The bridge swings open (at least 30 times a day) to let the seagoing ships pass through. The original bridge, built in 1888, was the brainchild of the American consul Leonard Burlington Smith, who made a mint off the tolls he charged for the bridge. Initially, the charge was 2¢ per person for those wearing shoes, free to those crossing barefoot. Today it's free to everyone.

Queen Juliana Bridge. This 1,625-ft-long bridge, to the north of the Queen Emma Bridge, was completed in 1974 and stands 200 ft above water—a great vantage point for photos of the city. It's the bridge you drive over to cross to the other side of the city, and although the route is time-consuming (and more expensive if you're going by taxi), the view is worth it. At every hour of the day, the sun casts a different tint over the city; the nighttime view, rivaling Rio's, is breathtaking.

Scharloo. The Wilhelmina Drawbridge connects Punda with the once-flourishing district of Scharloo, where the early Jewish merchants first built stately homes. The end of the district closest to Kleine Werf is now a red-light district and is pretty run down, but the rest of the area is well worth a visit. The architecture along Scharlooweg (much of it dating from the 17th century) is intriguing and many of the structures have been meticulously renovated.

Beaches

Curaçao has some 38 beaches, but unfortunately some are rocky and litter-strewn. The best way to find "your" beach is to rent a Jeep, motor scooter, or heavy-treaded car. Curaçao doesn't have Aruba's long stretches of sand; instead, you'll discover the joy of inlets: tiny bay openings to the sea marked by craggy cliffs, exotic trees, and scads of interesting pebbles. Imagine a beach that's just big enough for two. Beware of thorns and keep an eye out for flying fish. They propel their tails through the water until they reach a speed of 44 mph, then spread their fins and soar.

Curaçao has facilities for all kinds of water sports, thanks to the government-sponsored **Curaçao Underwater Marine Park** (☞ Exploring, *above*), which includes almost a third of the island's southern diving waters. No coral collecting, spearfishing, or littering is allowed. And remember, do not scuba dive if you will be flying within 24 hours.

Hotels with the best beaches include the Sonesta Beach Hotel (impressively long); the Princess Beach (impressively sensuous); and the Lions Dive Beach Resort on the Seaquarium Beach (impressive for its amenities). Beach-hopping to other hotels can be fun: Nonguests are supposed to pay the hotels a beach fee, but often there is no one to collect.

Daai Booi Bay is a sandy shore dotted with thatched shelters. The road to this public beach (follow signs from the church of St. Willibrordus) is a small paved highway flanked by thick lush trees and huge organ-pipe cacti. The beach is curved, with shrubbery rooted into the side of the rocky cliffs—a great place for swimming. **Knip Bay** has two parts: Big (Groot) Knip and Little (Kleine) Knip. Only Little Knip is shaded with trees, but these are manchineels, so steer clear of them. Also beware of cutting your feet on beer-bottle caps. Both beaches have alluring white sand, but only Big Knip has changing facilities. Big Knip also has several tiki huts for shade and calm turquoise waters that are perfect for swimming and lounging. The protected cove, flanked by sheer cliffs, is usually a blast on Sunday, when there is occasionally live music. To get there, take the road to the Knip Landhouse, then turn right. Signs will direct you. **Playa Abao,** northwest of Knip Bay, has crystal-clear turquoise water and a small beach. Sunday afternoons are crowded and festive. There's a snack bar and public toilets. **Westpunt,** on the northwest tip of the island, is shady in the morning. It doesn't have much sand, but you can sit on a shaded rock ledge. On Sunday, watch the divers jump from the high cliff. The bay view is worth the trip. **Playa Lagun,** southeast of Playa Forti, is dotted with powder-blue camping huts and caught between towering gunmetal gray cliffs. Cognoscenti know this is one of the best places to snorkel—you may even go nose to nose with the resident giant squid.

You'll pay a fee ($2.25 per person) to enter **Seaquarium's Beach,** but the amenities (rest rooms, showers, boutiques, water-sports center, snack bar, restaurant with beach bar, thatched shelters and palm trees for shade, security patrols, even a calling station to call or fax home) on this 500-meter man-made beach and calm waters protected by a breakwater are well worth it. Top Watersports Curaçao (☎ 5999/461–7343) rents water scooters ($45–$60), canoes ($6–$8), snorkel gear ($12), and floating mats ($3) here. **Santa Barbara,** a popular family beach on the eastern tip, is reached by driving through one of Curaçao's toniest neighborhoods, Spanish Water, where gleaming white yachts replace humble fishing fleets. The beach has changing facilities and a snack bar but charges a small admission fee, usually around $2.25 per person. Around the bend, **Caracas Bay** is a popular dive site, with a sunken ship so close to the surface that snorkelers can view it clearly.

Dining

Dine under the boughs of magnificent old trees, in the romantic gloom of wine cellars in renovated landhouses, or on the ramparts of 18th-century forts. Curaçaoans partake of some of the best Indonesian food in the Caribbean, and you'll also find fine French, Swiss, Dutch, and Swedish fare.

What to Wear

Dress in restaurants is almost always casual (though beachwear is generally not acceptable). Some of the resort dining rooms and nicer restaurants require that men wear jackets, especially in high season; ask when you make reservations. Do take a wrap or a light sweater with you—most restaurants keep air conditioners at full blast.

CATEGORY	COST*
$$$$	over $40
$$$	$30–$40
$$	$15–$30
$	under $15

*per person for a three-course meal, excluding drinks and service charge

$$$$ ✕ **Dee Taveerne.** From the intricate detail of its antiques
★   and brickwork to its impressive Continental menu, this restaurant is the most elegant, romantic spot on the island. You'll dine in the whitewashed wine cellar of a magnificent renovated octagonal country estate, built in the 1800s by an exiled Venezuelan revolutionary. The best appetizer is the salmon carpaccio with laurel bay dressing en brioche. The entrées are rich and decadent: velvety lobster bisque finished with Armagnac, sautéed goose liver in plum sauce, smoked eel with horseradish. ⊠ *Landhuis Groot Davelaar, on Silena, near Promenade Shopping Center,* ☎ *5999/ 737–0669. AE, D, DC, MC, V. Closed Sun.*

$$$–$$$$ ✕ **Bistro Le Clochard.** This romantic gem is built into the 18th-century Rif Fort—an oasis of arched entryways, exposed brickwork, wood beams, and lace curtains. Cocktails and hors d'oeuvres are served on the Waterside Terrace, with its view of the floating bridge and harbor. The French and Swiss dishes are consistently well prepared, though pricey. Try the fresh-fish platters or the veal in mushroom sauce. Savor the fondue and save room for the chocolate mousse. Avoid weekends, when an inexplicably corny duo plays, but you might enjoy

Pick up
the phone.

Pick up
the miles.

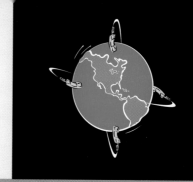

Use your MCI Card® to make an international call from virtually anywhere in the world and earn frequent flyer miles on one of seven major airlines.

Enroll in an MCI Airline Partner Program today. In the U.S., call **1-800-FLY-FREE.** Overseas, call MCI collect at **1-916-567-5151.**

1. To use your MCI Card, just dial the WorldPhone access number of the country you're calling from.
   (For a complete listing of codes, visit www.mci.com.)
2. Dial or give the operator your MCI Card number.
3. Dial or give the number you're calling.

# American Samoa	633-2MCI (633-2624)
# Antigua (Available from public card phones only)	#2
# Argentina (CC)	0800-5-1002
# Aruba ÷	800-888-8
# Bahamas	1-800-888-8000
# Barbados	1-800-888-8000
# Belize	557 from hotels
	815 from pay phones
# Bermuda ÷	1-800-888-8000
# Bolivia ♦	0-800-2222
# Brazil (CC)	000-8012
# British Virgin Islands ÷	1-800-888-8000
# Cayman Islands	1-800-888-8000
# Chile (CC)	
To call using CTC ■	800-207-300
To call using ENTEL ■	800-360-180
# Colombia (CC) ♦	980-16-0011
Columbia IIIC Access in Spanish	980-16-1000
# Costa Rica ♦	0800-012-2222
# Dominica	1-800-888-8000
# Dominican Republic (CC) ÷	1-800-888-8000
Dominican Republic IIIC Access in Spanish	1121
# Ecuador (CC) ÷	999-170
El Salvador ♦	800-1767
# Grenada ÷	1-800-888-8000
Guatemala (CC) ♦	9999-189

# Guyana	177
# Haiti (CC) ÷	193
Haiti IIIC Access in French/Creole	190
Honduras ÷	122
# Jamaica ÷	1-800-888-8000
(From Special Hotels only)	873
# Mexico	
Avantel (CC)	91-800-021-8000
Telmex ▲	95-800-674-7000
Mexico IIIC Access	91-800-021-1000
# Netherlands Antilles (CC) ÷	001-800-888-8000
Nicaragua (CC)	166
(Outside of Managua, dial 02 first)	
Nicaragua IIIC Access in Spanish	★2 from any public pay phone
# Panama	108
Military Bases	2810-108
# Paraguay ÷	008-112-800
# Peru (CC)	0-800-500-10
# Puerto Rico (CC)	1-800-888-8000
# St. Lucia ÷	1-800-888-8000
# Trinidad & Tobago ÷	1-800-888-8000
# Turks & Caicos ÷	1-800-888-8000
# Uruguay	000-412
# U.S. Virgin Islands (CC)	1-800-888-8000
# Venezuela (CC) ÷ ♦	800-1114-0

Is this a great time, or what? :-)

Urban planning.

CITYPACKS

The ultimate guide to the city—a complete pocket guide plus a full-size color map.

the complimentary snacks of Friday's 5-to-7 Hungry Hour. ⊠ *On the Otrabanda, Rif Fort,* ☎ *5999/462–5666. AE, DC, MC, V. Closed Sun. No lunch Sat.*

$$$ ✕ **Fort Nassau Restaurant.** This is *the* place to view twinkling Curaçao at night. High on a hilltop overlooking Willemstad, the restaurant is built into an 18th-century fort with a 360-degree view. Go for a drink in the breezy Battery Terrace bar or dine in air-conditioned comfort in front of the huge bay windows. The menu is diverse, from rabbit, duck, pigeon, and beef preparations to lightly broiled fish (ask the waiter what's fresh). Stay away from the enticing yet overly complex stabs at innovative cuisine: The simple selections are best here. Dinner seatings are at 7 and 9 PM. ⊠ *Schottengatweg 82, near Juliana Bridge,* ☎ *5999/ 461–3450. Reservations essential. AE, D, DC, MC, V. No lunch weekends.*

$$$ ✕ **La Pergola.** Built into the stuccoed walls of the Waterfort Arches, with huge picture windows fronting the rambunctious sea and a pretty pink-and-white arbor wound with bunches of grapes, La Pergola offers creative variations on Italian standards. Try the smoked salmon drizzled with olive oil and studded with cloves or the grouper siciliana with capers, olives, anchovies, tomatoes, and garlic. Pizza reigns supreme (13 choices) on the terrace menu. ⊠ *Waterfort Arches, Willemstad,* ☎ *5999/461–3482. AE, DC, MC, V. No lunch Sun.*

$$–$$$ ✕ **Pirates.** A friendly and efficient wait staff delivers dish after dish of superb seafood, including oyster soup, seviche, paella, and conch. The sea bass Creole-style is delicious, as is the red snapper in almond sauce. The decor is nautical (if somewhat hokey), with an anchor, a watch tower, and, of course, a mermaid. ⊠ *Curaçao Caribbean Hotel,* ☎ *5999/ 462–8500. AE, DC, MC, V.*

$$ ✕ **Fort Waakzaamheid Tavern.** High on a hill overlooking Willemstad and the harbor, this fort was captured by Captain Bligh of HMS *Bounty* two centuries ago. The open-air restaurant and bar is informal, and the food is primarily barbecued seafood and steaks decorated with your own makings from a salad bar. You will be equally well greeted if you go just for cocktails and snacks—and the sunsets are magnificent. ⊠ *Off main highway on Otrabanda side of suspension bridge, Seru Domi, Willemstad,* ☎ *5999/462– 3633. AE, D, MC, V. Closed Tues. No lunch.*

$$ ✕ **Mambo Beach.** On the west end of Seaquarium Beach (and we do mean *on* the beach), Mambo Beach is a hip, open-air bar and grill spread over the sand that serves surprisingly good food for breakfast, lunch, and dinner. Baguettes dominate the lunch menu, while steaks, fresh seafood, and pasta fill the dinner menu. This is a fantastic place to watch the setting sun, but don't forget your insect repellent and apply it liberally. ⊠ *Seaquarium Beach,* ☎ *5999/461–8999. AE, MC, V.*

$$ ✕ **Rijstaffel Indonesia Restaurant.** An antique rickshaw
★ guarding the entrance sets the mood in this tranquil spot. No steaks or chops served here, just exotic delicacies that make up the traditional Indonesian banquet called rijsttafel, where some 16 to 25 dishes are set buffet-style around you. Smaller appetites should opt for the *nasi rames,* a mini-version with only eight dishes. Vegetarians will be pleased that a 16-course vegetable rijsttafel is also available. An à la carte menu includes fried noodles, fresh jumbo shrimp in garlic, and combination meat-and-fish platters. ⊠ *Mercurriusstraat 13–15, Salina,* ☎ *5999/461–2606. AE, DC, MC, V. No lunch Sun.*

$$ ✕ **Seaview.** This casual terrace eatery is nestled snugly in the corner of the Waterfort Arches, where the surf pounds against the rocks—you expect the sea to drench you at any minute. Try the tender pepper fillet or the tangy *salpicon de mariscos,* a version of seviche that includes everything from octopus to shrimp vinaigrette. The chef also creates such specialties as green-and-white asparagus en brioche. It's a great place to watch the pyrotechnics of the sun at dusk. ⊠ *Waterfort Arches, Willemstad,* ☎ *5999/461–6688. AE, DC, MC, V. No lunch Sun.*

$ ✕ **Cactus Club.** A veritable grove of aloe and cacti greets you in the courtyard of this Caribbean version of Bennigan's. The inside is surprisingly subdued: faux Tiffany lamps, hanging plants, whirring ceiling fans. Food is cheap and filling, including fettuccine Alfredo, fajitas, buffalo wings, and Cajun snapper. It's popular with both locals and homesick Americans. ⊠ *Van Staverenweg 6,* ☎ *5999/737–1600. DC, MC, V.*

$ ✕ **Café du Port.** This alfresco harborfront café serves baguette sandwiches—the salmon salad and pâté are good choices—and cold drinks, from shakes and sodas to fancier alcohol-infused libations. Egg dishes and ham and Dutch cheese are available for breakfast. It's a scenic little spot to cool off with a drink; the view of the floating bridge is splendid. ⊠ *Handelskade 13, Punda,* ☎ *5999/465–0670. AE, MC, V.*

$ ✗ **Golden Star Restaurant.** This place looks and feels more like a friendly roadside diner, but the native food here is among the best in town. Owner Marie Burke turns out such Antillean specialties as *bestia chiki* (goat stew), shrimp Creole, and delicately seasoned grilled conch, with generous heaps of rice, fried plantains, and avocado. ⊠ *Socratestraat 2,* ☎ *5999/461– 8828. AE, DC, MC, V. Closed Tues.*

$ ✗ **Jaanchi's Restaurant.** Tour buses stop at this open-air
★ restaurant for lunches of mouthwatering Curaçaoan dishes. The main-course specialty is a hefty platter of fresh-caught fish, conch, or shrimp with potatoes or *funchi* (corn bread) and vegetables. You can also try stewed goat here. Curaçaoans joke that Jaanchi's "iguana soup is so strong it could resurrect the dead"—truth is, it tastes just like chicken soup, only better. But Jaanchi Jr. says, if you want iguana, you should order in advance "because we have to go out and catch them." He's not kidding. He usually closes at 6:30 PM but will stay open later if you call ahead to reserve a spot. ⊠ *Westpunt 15,* ☎ *5999/864–0126. AE, DC, MC, V.*

Shopping

Curaçao has long enjoyed the reputation of having some of the best shops in the Caribbean, with classier displays and a better variety than on many islands, but don't expect posh Madison Avenue boutiques. With a few exceptions (such as at Benetton, which recently moved into the Caribbean with a vengeance), the quality of women's fashions here lies along the lines of sales racks. Many shops are closed on Monday and virtually all lock up by 6 PM the remainder of the week. If you're looking for bargains on Swiss watches, cosmetics, cameras, crystal, perfumes, Nike or Reebok sneakers, or electronic equipment, do some comparison shopping back home and come armed with a list of prices. Willemstad is no longer a free port: there's now a tax and consequently prices are higher.

Shopping Areas

Most of the shops are concentrated in Willemstad's Punda within about a six-block area. The main shopping streets are Heerenstraat, Breedestraat, and Madurostraat. Heeren-

straat and Gomezplein are pedestrian malls, closed to traffic, and their roadbeds have been raised to sidewalk level
and covered with pink inlaid tiles.

Good Buys

Bamali (✉ Breedestraat 2, ☎ 5999/461–2258) sells Indonesian batik clothing, leather bags, and charming
handicrafts. **Boolchand's** (✉ Heerenstraat 4B, ☎ 5999/461–
2262) handles an interesting variety of merchandise behind
a facade of red-and-white-checked tiles. Stock up here on
French perfumes, British cashmere sweaters, Italian silk ties,
Dutch dolls, Swiss watches, and Japanese cameras. **Julius
L. Penha & Sons** (✉ Heerenstraat 1, ☎ 5999/461–2266),
in front of the Pontoon Bridge, sells French perfumes,
Hummel figurines, linen from Madeira, delftware, and
handbags from Argentina, Italy, and Spain. The store also
has an extensive cosmetics counter. **Little Switzerland** (✉
Breedestraat 44, ☎ 5999/461–2111) is the place for duty-
free shopping; you'll find perfumes, jewelry, watches, crystal, china, and leather goods at significant savings. **Sparky's**
(✉ Braastraat 23, ☎ 5999/461–7462) carries all the major
brands of cosmetics and perfume.

CLOTHING

Benetton (✉ Madurostraat 4, ☎ 5999/461–4619, and
other locations) has winter stock in July and summer stock
in December; all of it is 20% off the retail price. **Boutique
Aquarius** (✉ Breedestraat 9, ☎ 5999/461–2618) sells Fendi
merchandise for 25% less than in the United States. Fendi
fanatics can stock up on belts, shoes, pocketbooks, wallets,
and even watches. **Boutique Liska** (✉ Schottegatweg Oost
191-A, ☎ 5999/461–3111) draws local residents shopping
for smart women's fashions. **Clog Dance** (✉ De Rouvilleweg
9B, ☎ 5999/462–3280) is where to go if you long for
Dutch clogs, cheeses, tulips, delftware, Dutch fashions, or
chocolate. **Crazy Look** (✉ Madurostraat 32, ☎ 5999/461–
1440) has hip French, Italian, and Dutch fashions, as well
as trendy sweatshirts and baggy pants. For the latest European shoes to go with a funky new outfit, visit **Cinderella**
(✉ Haaranstraat 4, ☎ 5999/461–5000).

DELICACIES

Toko Zuikertuintje (✉ Zuikertuintjeweg, ☎ 5999/737–
0188), a supermarket built on the original 17th-century

Zuikertuintje Landhuis, is where most of the local elite shop for all sorts of European and Dutch delicacies. Shopping here for a picnic is a treat in itself.

JEWELRY AND WATCHES

Gandelman (⊠ Breedestraat 35, ☎ 5999/461–1854; ⊠ Sonesta Beach Hotel, ☎ 5999/462–8386) has watches by Cartier and Piaget, leather goods by Prima Classe, and Baccarat and Daum crystal. **La Zahav N.V.** (⊠ Curaçao International Airport, ☎ 5999/868–9594) is one of the best places to buy gold jewelry—with or without diamonds, rubies, and emeralds—at true discount prices. The shop is in the airport transit hall, just at the top of the staircase.

LINENS

New Amsterdam (⊠ Gomezplein 14, ☎ 5999/461–2469) is the place to price hand-embroidered tablecloths, napkins, and pillowcases. Tablecloths begin at $35, double bedspreads at $100.

LOCAL CRAFTS

Arawak Craft Factory (⊠ Cruise Terminal, Otrabanda, ☎ 5999/462–7249) has a factory showroom of native-made crafts. You can purchase a variety of tiles, plates, pots, and tiny replicas of landhouses. **Black Koral** (⊠ Princess Beach Hotel, ☎ 5999/465–2122) is owned by Dutch-born artisan Bert Knubben, one of Curaçao's true characters. For the past 30 years, he's been designing and sculpting the most exciting black-coral jewelry in the Caribbean—and he even dives for the coral himself, with special permission from the government. Dolphin pendants and twiglike earrings finished in 14-karat gold are excellent buys. Call before you drop by. **Fundason Obra di Man** (⊠ Bargestraat 57, Punda, ☎ 5999/461–2413) stocks native crafts and curios. Particularly impressive are the posters of Curaçao's architecture. **Kas di Arte Kursou** (⊠ Breedestraat 126, Otrabanda, ☎ 5999/864–2516) carries a variety of handmade souvenirs. **Gallery 86** (⊠ Trompstraat, Punda, ☎ 5999/461–3417) features the works of local artists and occasionally those of South Americans and Africans. **Landhuis Groot Santa Martha** (⊠ Santa Martha, ☎ 5999/864–1559) is where artisans with disabilities fashion handicrafts of varying types.

Curaçao A to Z

Arriving and Departing

BY PLANE

Aruba and Curaçao are a quick ½-hour journey apart (you'll be airborne for only 15 minutes). **ALM** (☎ 5999/869–5533 or 800/327–7230), Curaçao's national airline, and **Air Aruba** (☎ 5999/868–3777 or 800/882–7822) have daily flights to and from Curaçao; a round-trip fare cost $106 at press time. **E Liner Airways** (☎ 5999/465–8099 or 5999/560–4773) also has interisland service. For tour packages to Curaçao that include flight arrangements, *see* Guided Tours, *below.*

Currency

U.S. dollars—in cash or traveler's checks—are accepted nearly everywhere, so there's no need to worry about exchanging money. However, you may need small change for pay phones, cigarettes, or soda machines. The currency in the Netherlands Antilles is the guilder, or florin, as it is also called, indicated by an fl or Naf on price tags. Don't confuse it with the Aruban florin (AFl). The U.S. dollar is considered very stable; the official rate of exchange at press time was NAf1.77 to the U.S. $1. Note: Prices quoted here are in U.S. dollars unless indicated otherwise.

Getting Around

CAR RENTALS

You can rent a car from **Budget** (☎ 5999/868–3466 or 800/472–3325), **Avis** (☎ 5999/461–1255 or 800/331–1212), **Dollar** (☎ 5999/461–3144), or **National Car Rental** (☎ 5999/868–3489 or 800/328–4567) at the airport. Rates typically range from about $60 a day for a Toyota Tercel to about $75 for a four-door sedan or four-wheel drive; add 6% tax and required $10 daily insurance. If you're planning to do country driving or rough it through Christoffel Park, a four-wheel drive is best.

TAXIS

Taxi drivers have an official tariff chart, with fares from the airport vicinity to Willemstad and the nearby beach hotels running about $10–$15, $30–$40 to hotels in the west end of the island. Taxis tend to be moderately priced, but since there are no meters, you should confirm the fare with the driver before departure. There is an additional 25% surcharge after 11 PM. Taxis are readily available at hotels; in other cases, call Central Dispatch at ☎ 5999/869–0747.

Guided Tours

A guided tour can save you time and energy, though it is easy to cover the island yourself in a rented car. If you didn't book a package tour from Aruba, most hotels in Curaçao have tour desks where arrangements can be made with reputable tour operators.

Casper Tours (☎ 5999/465–3010) has very personal, amiable service. For around $25 per person, you'll be escorted around the island in an air-conditioned van, with stops at the Juliana Bridge, the salt lakes, Knip Bay for a swim, the grotto at Boca Tabla, and Jaanchi's Restaurant—famous for its native cuisine—for lunch (not included). **Curven Tours** (☎ 5999/737–9806) offers island tours and special packages to Venezuela. **DePalm Tours** (☎ 297/8–24400 or 800/766–6016) provides round-trip transportation from Aruba on its Curaçao tour, which takes place on Thursday only. You'll be picked up from your hotel at 6:30 AM and returned 12 hours later. Tour stops include Boca Tabla, Westpunt, the Seaquarium, lunch at the Sonesta Hotel, and shopping in Willemstad. The cost is $209 per person, and reservations must be made by the prior Tuesday at noon. Most hotels will be able to make the arrangements for you. For more information *see* Orientation Tours *in* Chapter 7. **SEAruba Fly 'n Dive** (☎ 297/8–38759 or 297/9–32822) is based in Aruba and can tailor a one-, two-, or three-day Curaçao trip to your desire. Dive instructor and pilot John Oster will be your guide. Prices vary but run about $250 per person. **Shorex** (☎ 5999/462–8833) books a variety of entertaining island tours, including the Willemstad Trolley Train Tour ($15), which passes all the major downtown sights in an hour, and Eastern Highlights, a five-hour tour that visits Curaçao Ostrich Farm, Fort Nassau, an herb garden, and Landhuis Jan Thiel ($27). **Taber Tours** (☎ 5999/737–6637) offers a three-hour East Tour ($13) that includes visits to the Curaçao Liqueur Factory at Landhuis Chobolobo, the Curaçao Museum, and the Bloempot shopping center. For personalized history and nature tours, contact **Dornasol Tours** (☎ 5999/868–2735); half-day tours run $25 and full-day tours are $40 per person.

BOAT TOURS

Seaworld Explorer (☎ 5999/462–8833), a semisubmersible, runs hour-long tours of the island's beautiful coral reefs ($30). Many sailboats and motorboats offer comparably priced sunset cruises ($30), snorkel trips ($25), and day-long snorkel and picnic trips to Klein Curaçao ($50), the "clothes optional" island between Curaçao and Bonaire. Top choices among the many boats are the 90-ft, turbo-driven *Waterworld* (☎ 5999/465–6042), the twin-masted sailboat *Vira Cocha* (☎ 5999/560–0292), the 120-ft Dutch sailing ketch *Insulinde* (☎ 5999/560–1340), and the 90-ft schooner *Bounty* (☎ 5999/560–1887).

Language

Dutch is the official language but, as in Aruba, the vernacular is Papiamento—a mixture of Dutch, African, French, Portuguese, Spanish, and English. English as well as Spanish—and, of course, Dutch—are studied by schoolchildren. Anyone involved with tourism—shopkeepers, restaurateurs, and museum guides—speaks English.

Opening and Closing Times

Most shops are open Monday–Saturday 8–noon and 2–6. Banks are open weekdays 8–3:30 or 8–11:30 and 1:30–4.

Passports and Visas

U.S. and Canadian citizens traveling to Curaçao need only proof of citizenship and a valid photo ID. A voter's registration card or a notarized birth certificate (not a photocopy) will suffice—a driver's license will *not*. British citizens must produce a passport. All visitors must show an ongoing or return ticket.

Precautions

Mosquitoes definitely exist on Curaçao, at least during the rainy season. The bad news is the rainy season falls between November and April, coinciding with the tourist high season. To be safe, keep perfume to a minimum, be prepared to use insect repellent before dining alfresco.

If you plan to go into the water, beware of long-spined sea urchins, which can be painful if you come in contact with them.

Do not eat any of the little green applelike fruits (they even smell like apples) of the manchineel tree: They're poisonous. In fact, steer clear of the trees altogether; raindrops or dewdrops dripping off the leaves can blister your skin. If contact does occur, rinse the affected area with water and, in extreme cases, get medical attention. Usually, the burning sensation won't last longer than two hours.

Crime is on the increase in Curaçao, so common-sense rules apply. Lock rental cars, use the theft deterrent device if provided by the rental firm, and do not leave valuables in the car. Never leave bags unattended at the airport, on tours, or on the beach.

Taxes and Service Charges

Restaurants add a 10%–15% tax and service charge to the bill. Most shops and restaurants also tack on 6% ABB tax (a new value-added tax aimed specifically at tourists). The airport international departure tax is NAf122.50 or $12.50.

Telephones and Mail

To call Curaçao direct from the United States, dial 011–5999 plus the number in Curaçao. To place a local call on the island, dial the seven-digit local number. An airmail letter to the United States, Canada, or the United Kingdom costs NAf2.25, a postcard NAf1.25.

Visitor Information

Contact the **Curaçao Tourist Board** (✉ 475 Park Ave. S, Suite 2000, New York, NY 10016, ☎ 212/683–7660 or 800/270–3350, FAX 212/683–9337; ✉ 330 Biscayne Blvd., Suite 808, Miami, FL 33132, ☎ 305/374–5811 or 800/445–8266, FAX 305/374–6741 for information).

In Curaçao, the **Curaçao Tourism Development Foundation** has two offices on the island where multilingual guides are ready to answer questions. You can also pick up maps, brochures, and a copy of *Curaçao Holiday*. The main office is in Willemstad at Pietermaai No. 19 (☎ 5999/461–6000); the other is at the airport (☎ 5999/868–6789).

9 A Gambling Primer

HERE'S A SHORT-FORM HANDBOOK on the rules, the plays, the odds, and the strategies for the most popular casino games. When you decide what kind of action you want to pursue, choose a game that best suits your style.

THE GOOD BETS

The first part of any viable casino strategy is to risk the most money on wagers that present the lowest edge for the house. Blackjack, craps, video poker, and baccarat are the most advantageous to the bettor in this regard. The two types of bets at baccarat have a house advantage of a little more than 1%. The basic line bets at craps, if backed up with full odds, can be as low as .5%. Blackjack and video poker can, at times, not only put you even with the house (a true 50-50 proposition) but also actually give you a slight long-term advantage.

How can a casino possibly provide you with a 50-50 or even a positive expectation at some of its games? First, because a vast number of suckers make the bad bets (those with a house advantage of 5%–35%, such as roulette, keno, and slots) day in and day out. Second, because the casino knows that very few people are aware of the opportunities to beat the odds. Third, because it takes skill—requiring study and practice—to be in a position to exploit the opportunities the casino presents. However, a mere hour or two spent learning strategies for the beatable games will put you light years ahead of the vast majority of visitors, who give the gambling industry an average 12%–15% profit margin.

Baccarat

The most "glamorous" game in the casino, baccarat (pronounced *bah*-kuh-rah) is a version of chemin de fer, popular in European gambling halls, and is a favorite with high rollers, because thousands of dollars are often staked on one hand. The Italian word *baccara* means "zero"; this refers to the point value of 10s and picture cards. The game is run by four pit personnel. Two dealers sit side by side in the middle of the table; they handle the winning and losing bets and keep track of each player's "commission" (explained below). The "caller" stands in the middle of the other side of the table and dictates the action. The ladderman supervises the game and acts as final judge if any disputes arise.

How to Play

Baccarat is played with eight decks of cards dealt from a large "shoe" (or cardholder). Each player is offered a turn at handling the shoe and dealing the cards. Two two-card hands are dealt, the "player" and the "bank" hands. The player who deals the cards is called the banker, though the house, of course, banks both hands. The players bet on which hand, player or banker, will come closest to totaling 9 (a "natural"). The cards are valued as follows: ace through 9 retain face value, while 10s and picture cards are worth zero. If you have a hand adding up to more than 10, the number 10 is subtracted from the total. For example, if one hand contains a 10 and a 4, the hand adds up to 4. If the other holds an ace and a 6, it adds up to 7. If a hand has a 7 and a 9, it adds up to 6.

Depending on the two hands, the caller either declares a winner and loser (if either hand actually adds up to 8 or 9) or calls for another card for the player hand (if it totals 1, 2, 3, 4, 5, or 10). The bank hand then either stands pat or draws a card, determined by a complex series of rules depending on what the player's total is and dictated by the caller. When one or the other hand is declared a winner, the dealers go into action to pay off the winning wagers, collect the losing wagers, and add up the commission (usually 5%) that the house collects on the bank hand. Both bets have a house advantage of slightly more than 1%.

The player-dealer (or banker) continues to hold the shoe as long as the bank hand wins. As soon as the player hand wins, the shoe moves counterclockwise around the table. Players are not required to deal; they can refuse the shoe and pass it to the next player. Because the caller dictates the action, the player's responsibilities are minimal. It's not necessary to know any of the card-drawing rules, even if you're the banker.

Baccarat Strategy

Making a bet at baccarat is very simple: You place your money in either the bank, the player, or the tie box on the layout, which appears directly in front of your seat at the table. If you're betting that the bank hand will win, you put your chips in the bank box; bets for the player hand go in the player box. (Only real suckers bet on the tie.) Most players bet on the bank hand when they deal, since they "represent" the bank and to do otherwise would seem as if they were betting against themselves. This isn't really true, but it seems that way. In the end, playing baccarat is a simple matter of guessing whether the player or banker hand will come closest to 9 and deciding how much to bet on the outcome.

Blackjack

Blackjack is the most popular table game in the casino. It's easy to learn and fun to play. It involves skill and therefore presents varying levels of challenge, from beginner to post-graduate. Blackjack also boasts one of the lowest house advantages. Because blackjack is the only table game in the casino in which players can gain a long-term advantage over the house, it is the only game in the casino (other than, to a limited degree, video poker) that can be played professionally. And because blackjack can be played professionally, it is the most written-about and discussed casino game. Of course, training someone to play blackjack professionally is beyond the scope of this guide. Contact the Gambler's Book Club (☎ 702/382–7555) for a catalog of gambling books, software, and videotapes, including the largest selection on blackjack around.

How to Play

Basically, here's how it works: You play blackjack against a dealer, and whichever of you comes closest to a card total of 21 is the winner. Number cards are worth their face value, picture cards are worth 10, and aces are worth either 1 or 11. (Hands with aces in them are known as soft hands. Always count the ace first as an 11; if you also have a 10, your total will be 21, not 11.) If the dealer has a 17 and you have a 16, you lose. If you have an 18 against a dealer's

17, you win (even money). If both you and the dealer have a 17, it's a tie (or, push) and no money changes hands. If you go over a total of 21 (or, bust), you lose immediately, even if the dealer also busts later in the hand. If your first two cards add up to 21 (a natural), you're paid 3 to 2. However, if the dealer also has a natural, it's a push. A natural beats a total of 21 achieved with more than two cards.

You're dealt two cards, either face down or face up, depending on the custom of the particular casino. The dealer also gives herself two cards, one face down and one face up (except in double-exposure blackjack, where both the dealer's cards are visible). Depending on your first two cards and the dealer's up card, you can **stand,** or refuse to take another card. You can **hit,** or take as many cards as you need until you stand or bust. You can **double down,** or double your bet and take one card. You can **split** a like pair; if you're dealt two 8s, for example, you can double your bet and play the 8s as if they're two hands. You can **buy insurance** if the dealer is showing an ace. Here you're wagering half your initial bet that the dealer *does* have a natural; if so, you lose your initial bet, but are paid 2 to 1 on the insurance (which means the whole thing is a push). You can **surrender** half your initial bet if you're holding a bad hand (known as a stiff) such as a 15 or 16 against a high card facing up, like a 9 or 10.

Blackjack Strategy

Playing blackjack is not only knowing the rules—it's also knowing *how* to play. Many people devote a great deal of time to learning complicated statistical schemes. However, if you don't have the time, energy, or inclination to get that seriously involved, the following basic strategies, which cover more than half the situations you'll face, should allow you to play the game with a modicum of skill and a paucity of humiliation:

- When your hand is a stiff (a total of 12, 13, 14, 15, or 16) and the dealer shows a 2, 3, 4, 5, or 6, always stand.

- When your hand is a stiff and the dealer shows a 7, 8, 9, 10, or ace, always hit.

- When you hold 17, 18, 19, or 20, always stand.

- When you hold a 10 or 11 and the dealer shows a 2, 3, 4, 5, 6, 7, 8, or 9, always double down.

- When you hold a pair of aces or a pair of 8s, always split.

- Never buy insurance.

Craps

Craps is a dice game played at a large rectangular table with rounded corners. Up to 12 players can crowd around the table, all standing. The layout is mounted at the bottom of a surrounding "rail," which prevents the dice from being thrown off the table and provides an opposite wall against which to bounce the dice. It can require up to four pit personnel to run an action-packed, fast-paced game of craps. Two dealers handle the bets made on either side of the layout. A "stickman" wields the long wooden "stick," curved at one end, which is used to move the dice around the table; the stickman also calls the number that's rolled and books the proposition bets made in the middle of the layout. The "boxman" sits between the two dealers and oversees the game; he or she settles any disputes about rules, payoffs, mistakes, and so on.

How to Play

To play, just stand at the table wherever you can find an open space. You can start betting casino chips immediately, but you have to wait your turn to be the shooter. The dice move around the table in a clockwise fashion: The person to your right shoots before you, the one to the left after you (the stickman will give you the dice at the appropriate time). When you're the shooter, it's important to roll the dice hard enough so they bounce off the end wall of the table; this ensures a random bounce and shows that you're not trying to control the dice with a "soft" roll.

Craps Strategy

Playing craps is fairly straightforward; betting on it is the complicated part. The basic concepts are as follows: If the first time the shooter rolls the dice, he or she turns up a 7 or 11, that's called a natural—an automatic win. If a 2, 3, or 12 come up on the first throw (called the come-out roll), that's termed craps—an automatic lose. Each of the numbers 4, 5, 6, 8, 9, or 10 on a first roll is known as a point: The shooter has to keep rolling the dice until that number comes up again. If a 7 turns up before the number does, that's another loser. Then, when either the point (the original number thrown) or a 7 is rolled, this is known as a decision; one is made on average every 3.3 rolls.

But "winning" and "losing" rolls of the dice are entirely relative in this game because there are two ways you can bet at craps: for the shooter or against the shooter. Betting "for" means that the shooter will "make his point" (win). Betting "against" means that the shooter will "seven out" (lose). (Either way, you're actually betting against the house, which books all wagers.) If you're betting "for" on the come-out, you'd place your chips on the layout's "pass line." If a 7 or 11 is rolled, you win even money. If a 2, 3, or 12 (craps) is rolled, you lose your bet. If you're betting "against" on the come-out, you place your chips in the "don't pass bar." A 7 or 11 loses, a 2, 3, or 12 wins. A shooter can bet for or against himself or herself, as well as for or against the other players.

There are also roughly two dozen wagers you can make on any single specific roll of the dice. Craps strategy books can give you the details on bets such as Come/Don't Come, Odds, Place, Buy, Big Six, Field, and Proposition.

Video Poker

Like blackjack, video poker is a game of strategy and skill, and at select times on select machines, the player actually holds the advantage, however slight, over the house. Unlike slot machines, you can determine the exact edge of video poker machines. Like slots, however, video poker machines are often tied into a progressive meter; when the jackpot total reaches high enough, you can beat the casino at its own game. The variety of video poker machines is already large, and it's growing steadily larger. All the different machines are played in similar fashion, but the strategies are different. This section deals only with straight-draw video poker.

How to Play

The schedule for the payback on winning hands is posted on the machine, usually above the screen. It lists the returns for a high pair (generally jacks or better), two pairs, three of a kind, a flush, a full house, a straight flush, four of a kind, and a royal flush, depending on the number of coins played—usually 1, 2, 3, 4, or 5. Look for machines that pay with a single coin played: one coin for "jacks or better" (meaning a pair of jacks, queens, kings, or aces; any other pair is a "stiff"), two coins for two pairs, three for three of a kind, six for a flush, nine for a full house, 50 for a straight flush, 100 for four of a kind, and 250 for a royal flush. This is known as a 9/6 machine—one that gives a nine-coin payback for a full house and a six-coin payback for a flush with one coin played. Other machines are known as 8/5 (8 for a full house, 5 for a flush), 7/5, and 6/5.

You want a 9/6 machine because it gives you the best odds: The return from a standard 9/6 straight-draw machine is 99.5%; you give up only half a percent to the house. An 8/5 machine returns 97.3%. On 6/5 machines, the figure drops to 95.1%, slightly less than roulette. Machines with varying paybacks are scattered throughout the casinos. In some you'll see an 8/5 machine right next to a 9/6, and someone will be blithely playing the 8/5 machine!

As with slot machines, it's always optimum to play the maximum number of coins to qualify for the jackpot. You insert five coins into the slot and press the "deal" button. Five cards appear on the screen—say, 5, J, Q, 5, 9. To hold the pair of 5s, you press the "hold" buttons under the first and fourth cards. The word HOLD appears underneath the two 5s. You then press the "draw" button (often the same button as "deal") and three new cards appear on the screen—say, 10, J, 5. You have three 5s; with five coins bet, the machine will give you 15 credits. Now you can press the "max bet" button: five units will be removed from your number of credits, and five new cards will appear on the screen. You repeat the hold and draw process; if you hit a winning hand, the proper payback will be added to your credits. Those who want coins rather than credit can hit the "cash out" button at any time. Some machines don't have credit counters and automatically dispense coins for a winning hand.

Video Poker Strategy

Like blackjack, video poker has a basic strategy that's been formulated by the computer simulation of hundreds of millions of hands. The most effective way to learn it is with a video poker computer program that deals the cards on your screen, then tutors you in how to play each hand properly. If you don't want to devote that much time to the study of video poker, memorizing these six rules will help you make the right decision for more than half the hands you'll be dealt:

- If you're dealt a completely stiff hand (no like cards and no picture cards), draw five new cards.

- If you're dealt a hand with no like cards but with one jack, queen, king, or ace, always hold onto the picture card; if you're dealt two different picture cards, hold both. But if you're dealt three different picture cards, only hold two (the two of the same suit, if that's an option).

- If you're dealt a pair, always hold it, no matter what the face value.

- Never hold a picture card with a pair of 2s through 10s.

- Never draw two cards to try for a straight or a flush.

- Never draw one card to try for an inside straight.

HOUSE ADVANTAGE

Roulette

Roulette is a casino game that utilizes a perfectly balanced wheel with 38 numbers (0, 00, and 1 through 36), a small white ball, a large layout with 11 betting options, and special "wheel chips." The layout organizes the 11 bets into six "inside" bets (the single numbers, or those closest to the dealer) and five "outside" bets (the grouped bets, or those closest to the players).

The dealer spins the wheel clockwise and the ball counterclockwise. When the ball slows, the dealer announces, "No more bets." The ball drops from the "back track" to the "bottom track," caroming off built-in brass barriers and bouncing in and out of the different cups in the wheel before settling into the cup of the winning number. Then the dealer places a marker on the number and scoops all the losing chips into his or her corner. Depending on how crowded the game is, the casino can count on roughly 50 spins of the wheel per hour.

How to Play

To buy in, place your cash on the layout near the wheel. Inform the dealer of the denomination of the individual unit you intend to play (usually 25¢ or $1, but can go as high as $500). Know the table limits (displayed on a sign in the dealer area)—don't ask for a 25¢ denomination if the minimum is $1. The dealer gives you a stack of wheel chips—a color different from those of all other players—and places a chip marker atop one of your wheel chips on the rim of the wheel to identify its denomination. Note that you must cash in your wheel chips at the roulette table before you leave the game. Only the dealer can verify how much they're worth.

Roulette Strategy

With **inside bets,** you can lay any number of chips (depending on the table limits) on a single number, 1 through 36, 0, or 00. If the number hits, your payoff is 35 to 1, for a return of $36. You could conceivably place a $1 chip on all 38 numbers, but the return of $36 would leave you $2 short, which is 5.26% of the $38 you bet and, not surprisingly, the house advantage. If you place a chip on the line between two numbers and one of those numbers hits, you're paid 17 to 1 for a return of $18 (again, $2 short of breaking even). Betting on three numbers returns 11 to 1, four numbers returns 8 to 1, five numbers pays 6 to 1 (this is the worst roulette bet, with a 7.89% disadvantage), and six numbers pays 5 to 1.

To place an **outside bet,** lay a chip on one of three "columns" at the lower end of the layout next to numbers 34, 35, and 36; this pays 2 to 1. A bet placed in the first 12, second 12, or third 12 boxes also pays 2 to 1. A bet on red or black, odd or even, and 1 through 18 or 19 through 36 pays off at even money, 1 to 1. If you think you can bet on red *and* black or odd *and* even in order to play roulette and drink for free all night, think again. The green 0 or 00, which falls outside these two basic categories, will come up on average once every 19 spins of the wheel.

Slot Machines

Around the turn of the century, Charlie Fey built the first mechanical slot in his San Francisco basement. Slot machine technology has exploded in the past 20 years, and now there are hundreds of models, which accept everything from pennies to specially minted $500 tokens. The major advance in the game, however, is the progressive jackpot. Banks of slots within a particular casino are connected by computer, and the jackpot total is displayed on a digital meter above the machines. Generally, the total increases by 5% of the wager. If you're playing a dollar machine, each time you pull the handle (or press the spin button), a nickel is added to the jackpot.

How to Play

To play, insert your penny, nickel, quarter, silver dollar, or dollar token into the slot at the far right edge of the machine. Pull the handle or press the spin button, then wait for the reels to spin and stop one by one and for the machine to determine whether you're a winner (occasionally) or a loser (the rest of the time). It's pretty simple—but because there are so many types of machines nowadays, be sure you know exactly how the one you're playing operates.

Slot Machine Strategy

The house advantage on slots varies widely from machine to machine, between 3% and 25%. Casinos that advertise a 97% payback are telling you that at least one of their slot machines has a house advantage of 3%. Which one? There's really no way of knowing. Generally, $1 machines pay back at a higher percentage than quarter or nickel machines. On the other hand, machines with smaller jackpots pay back more money more frequently, meaning that you'll be playing with more of your winnings.

One of the all-time great myths about slot machines is that a particular machine is "due" for a jackpot. Slots, like roulette, craps, keno, and Big Six, are subject to the Law of Independent Trials, which means the odds are permanently and unalterably fixed. If the odds of lining up three sevens on a 25¢ slot machine have been set by the casino at 1 in 10,000, then those odds remain 1 in 10,000 whether the three 7s have been hit three times in a row or not hit for 90,000 plays. Don't waste a lot of time playing a machine that you suspect is "ready," and don't think if someone hits a jackpot on a particular machine only minutes after you've finished playing on it that it was "yours."

INDEX

✗ = restaurant, 🏨 = hotel

NOTES

NOTES

NOTES

Fodor's Travel Publications

Available at bookstores everywhere, or call 1–800–533–6478, 24 hours a day.

Gold Guides

U.S.

Alaska	Florida	New Orleans	Seattle & Vancouver
Arizona	Hawai'i	New York City	The South
Boston	Las Vegas,	Pacific North Coast	U.S. & British
California	Reno, Tahoe	Philadelphia &	Virgin Islands
Cape Cod, Martha's	Los Angeles	the Pennsylvania	USA
Vineyard, Nantucket	Maine, Vermont,	Dutch Country	Virginia & Maryland
The Carolinas &	New Hampshire	The Rockies	Walt Disney World,
Georgia	Maui & Lāna'i	San Diego	Universal Studios
Chicago	Miami & the Keys	San Francisco	and Orlando
Colorado	New England	Santa Fe, Taos,	Washington, D.C.
		Albuquerque	

Foreign

Australia	Europe	Mexico	Provence &
Austria	Florence, Tuscany	Montréal &	the Riviera
The Bahamas	& Umbria	Québec City	Scandinavia
Belize & Guatemala	France	Moscow, St.	Scotland
Bermuda	Germany	Petersburg, Kiev	Singapore
Canada	Great Britain	The Netherlands,	South Africa
Cancún, Cozumel,	Greece	Belgium &	South America
Yucatán Peninsula	Hong Kong	Luxembourg	Southeast Asia
Caribbean	India	New Zealand	Spain
China	Ireland	Norway	Sweden
Costa Rica	Israel	Nova Scotia,	Switzerland
Cuba	Italy	New Brunswick,	Thailand
The Czech Republic &	Japan	Prince Edward Island	Toronto
Slovakia	London	Paris	Turkey
Eastern &	Madrid & Barcelona	Portugal	Vienna & the Danube
Central Europe			Valley

Special-Interest Guides

Adventures to Imagine	Great American	Kodak Guide to	Walt Disney World
Alaska Ports of Call	Learning Vacations	Shooting Great	for Adults
Ballpark Vacations	Great American	Travel Pictures	Weekends in
Caribbean Ports	Sports & Adventure	National Parks and	New York
of Call	Vacations	Seashores of the East	Wendy Perrin's
The Complete Guide	Great American	National Parks of	Secrets Every Smart
to America's	Vacations	the West	Traveler Should Know
National Parks	Great American	Nights to Imagine	Where Should We
Disney Like a Pro	Vacations for	Rock & Roll Traveler	Take the Kids?
Europe Ports of Call	Travelers with	Great Britain	California
Family Adventures	Disabilities	and Ireland	Where Should We
Fodor's Gay Guide	Halliday's New	Rock & Roll Traveler	Take the Kids?
to the USA	Orleans Food	USA	Northeast
Fodor's How to Pack	Explorer	Sunday in	Worldwide Cruises
	Healthy Escapes	San Francisco	and Ports of Call

Fodor's Special Series

Fodor's Best Bed & Breakfasts

America
California
The Mid-Atlantic
New England
The Pacific Northwest
The South
The Southwest
The Upper Great Lakes

Compass American Guides

Alaska
Arizona
Boston
Chicago
Colorado
Hawai'i
Hollywood
Idaho
Las Vegas
Maine
Manhattan
Minnesota
Montana
New Mexico
New Orleans
Oregon
Pacific Northwest
San Francisco
Santa Fe
South Carolina
South Dakota
Southwest
Texas
Utah
Virginia
Washington
Wine Country
Wisconsin
Wyoming

Citypacks

Amsterdam
Atlanta
Berlin
Chicago
Florence
Hong Kong
London
Los Angeles
Montréal
New York City
Paris
Prague
Rome
San Francisco
Tokyo
Venice
Washington, D.C.

Exploring Guides

Australia
Boston & New England
Britain
California
Canada
Caribbean
China
Costa Rica
Egypt
Florence & Tuscany
Florida
France
Germany
Greek Islands
Hawaii
Ireland
Israel
Italy
Japan
London
Mexico
Moscow & St. Petersburg
New York City
Paris

Prague
Provence
Rome
San Francisco
Scotland
Singapore & Malaysia
South Africa
Spain
Thailand
Turkey
Venice

Flashmaps

Boston
New York
San Francisco
Washington, D.C.

Fodor's Gay Guides

Los Angeles & Southern California
New York City
Pacific Northwest
San Francisco and the Bay Area
South Florida
USA

Pocket Guides

Acapulco
Aruba
Atlanta
Barbados
Budapest
Jamaica
London
New York City
Paris
Prague
Puerto Rico
Rome
San Francisco
Washington, D.C.

Languages for Travelers (Cassette & Phrasebook)

French
German

Italian
Spanish

Mobil Travel Guides

America's Best Hotels & Restaurants
California and the West
Great Lakes
Major Cities
Mid-Atlantic
Northeast
Northwest and Great Plains
Southeast
Southwest and South Central

Rivages Guides

Bed and Breakfasts of Character and Charm in France
Hotels and Country Inns of Character and Charm in France
Hotels and Country Inns of Character and Charm in Italy
Hotels and Country Inns of Character and Charm in Paris
Hotels and Country Inns of Character and Charm in Portugal
Hotels and Country Inns of Character and Charm in Spain

Short Escapes

Britain
France
Near New York City
New England

Fodor's Sports

Golf Digest's Places to Play
Skiing USA
USA Today The Complete Four Sport Stadium Guide

WHEREVER YOU TRAVEL, *H*ELP IS NEVER FAR AWAY.

From planning your trip to

providing travel assistance along

the way, American Express®

Travel Service Offices are

always there to help

you do more.